**WITHDRAWN
UTSA Libraries**

The Best of
ALEXANDER MACLAREN

The Best of
ALEXANDER MACLAREN

Edited, with an Introduction by
GAIUS GLENN ATKINS

Biography Index Reprint Series

 BOOKS FOR LIBRARIES PRESS
FREEPORT, NEW YORK

Copyright 1949 by Harper & Brothers
All rights reserved

Reprinted 1971 by arrangement with
Harper & Row, Publishers

INTERNATIONAL STANDARD BOOK NUMBER:
0-8369-8101-4

LIBRARY OF CONGRESS CATALOG CARD NUMBER:
74-179733

PRINTED IN THE UNITED STATES OF AMERICA
BY
NEW WORLD BOOK MANUFACTURING CO., INC.
HALLANDALE, FLORIDA 33009

Contents

Introduction   vii

1. THE MEASURE OF IMMEASURABLE POWER   3
   from *The God of the Amen*
2. GOD'S GUESTS   11
   from *Triumphant Certainties*
3. UNPOSSESSED POSSESSIONS   19
   from *Christ's Musts*
4. "AS I HAVE LOVED"   27
   from *Last Sheaves*
5. THE SECRET OF IMMORTAL YOUTH   35
   from *The Unchanging Christ*
6. RIVER AND ROCK   45
   from *The God of the Amen*
7. MEMORY, HOPE, AND EFFORT   55
   from *Christ's Musts*
8. A SONG OF FAITH   63
   from *Last Sheaves*
9. CHRIST'S MUSTS   71
   from *Christ's Musts*
10. THE SHELTERING WING   79
    from *Triumphant Certainties*
11. THE CHRISTIAN ATTITUDE TO SOCIAL SINS   87
    from *Christ's Musts*
12. MAHANAIM: THE TWO CAMPS   95
    from *Christ in the Heart*

CONTENTS

13. THE WARRIOR PEACE 103
    from *The Unchanging Christ*
14. THE GUIDING PILLAR 111
    from *The Unchanging Christ*
15. THE SINGERS BY THE SEA 119
    from *Last Sheaves*
16. ITTAI OF GATH 127
    from *Christ in the Heart*
17. CHRIST'S TOUCH 135
    from *Christ in the Heart*
18. DEATH, THE FRIEND 145
    from *Last Sheaves*
19. WITHOUT THE CAMP 153
    from *Last Sheaves*
20. WHAT LASTS 161
    from *Triumphant Certainties*

Introduction

Alexander Maclaren was born in Glasgow February 11, 1826. He died in Manchester, England, May 5, 1910. He had been for almost sixty-five years a minister of the Gospel. His entire and consecrated devotion to his vocation makes him the despair of the biographer. The settings of his life work were so relatively simple as to need no long telling. A biographer loves drama. The drama of Maclaren's life was outwardly in climbing his pulpit stairs, preaching the sermons in whose preparation he spent secluded hours. He lived more than almost any of the great preachers of his time between his study, his pulpit, his pen—or later his typewriter. He subdued action to thought, thought to utterance, and utterance to the Gospel. His life was his ministry; his ministry was his life. The travail and triumph of it were in his sermons. And how can one make a biography of sermons—sixty-five years of sermons?

The Maclarens were of Highland stock. Alexander's sermons are always from the Highlands—gloom and gleam, tenderness and sternness, a music of words, a sustained poetry of utterance, and always an encompassing of depth and space. There is heather in them and summits seen through Celtic, mystic vision. His accent, it was said, betrayed him. It had the Scottish strength of stressed consonants which gave it enduring quality.

David Maclaren, Alexander's father, was a Glasgow city merchant, himself a capable businessman and gifted lay preacher. The provisions of Scottish Baptist churches for a plural ministry made that possible; and their opposition to clerical castes and sacerdotalism. The father is said to have been gifted in exposition, a clear thinker and therefore clear in style, qualities his son inherited. In 1836 he left Glasgow for an important business position in Australia. His family remained in Glasgow under the administration of his wife, a woman remembered for the sweetness of her disposition, her keen intelligence, and her devotion. They attended Hope Street Baptist Chapel, and there Alexander was deeply influenced by his pastor, the Reverend James Patterson.

Carlyle [1] said that Alexander's desire for baptism and church membership was the result of his home nurture and that there is no record of

---

[1] *Alexander Maclaren, the Man and His Message,* Funk & Wagnalls Company, 1902.

any struggle. Maclaren himself, in a letter written much later, tells of a real inner struggle. He was troubled about the doctrine of election. If God had already decided for him the eternal issue of his life, nothing he could do would matter, and he felt deeply, he said, the enormity of his sins. But he found "peace and power in believing that Christ is the savior" in a revival meeting, and therein surrendered himself to the Christian life.

He was then a student in Glasgow High School, shy, patient, reflective, plodding and tirelessly industrious. His father, who had returned to Great Britain, and having a natural concern for his son's future, hoped as all good Scottish fathers did then, that his son would become a minister. He took him therefore to a clerical friend and asked whether there was the making of a minister in the boy. His friend with Scotch caution thought it possible. The family removed to London in 1842 and Alexander was matriculated at Stepney College. Stepney was a Baptist institution, and Alexander was enrolled as a student and candidate for the Baptist ministry. He did not impress the examiner too favorably. He was tall, shy, silent, and looked no older than his sixteen years.

Stepney could not then have been large either in number of its students or in its faculty, but its principals were capable and their influence upon their students direct and telling. Stepney was an affiliate, if that word is at all right, of the recently established London University. London University was substantially an examining board with power to grant degrees; that is, its students got their training where and how they could. The examinations set by the qualified officers of the university were the test of a student's fitness for a degree. Those who passed the examinations, which were really very searching, and received their degrees had to be sound scholars. They would compare favorably with the graduates of Oxford and Cambridge, save for the prestige of those ancient universities and the mellowing effect of residence in their enchanted halls and gardens.

The ultracautious minister consulted by Alexander's father, who thought the shy youth no more than a ministerial possibility, might as well have held his peace. Alexander Maclaren's vocation, as he himself, a consistent Calvinist, might have said, was divinely decreed. "I can not," he said, "ever recall any hesitation as to being a minister. . . . It just had to be." All the forces of inheritance, home training, religious faith, and the prophetic urgings of his genius, combined to accentuate his call. Dr. Benjamin Davis was then principal of Stepney, and under his influence Alexander was thoroughly grounded in Greek and Hebrew.

He was taught to study the Bible "in the original," and so the foundation was laid not only for his distinctive work as an "expositor" but for the Biblical content and control of his preaching. There is no record of the detail of his homiletic training. One assumes that it was both specialized and thorough. He was never an extensive or brilliant letter writer, and few of his earlier letters have been preserved. Such as are preserved report him as comfortable and well-fed. He was apparently trained for preaching rather by process of absorption than by any departmental homiletic training. He was given a degree, certainly, in arts, in November, 1845. He won a first in the examination for "Theological Honours" and five pounds worth of books.[2]

Most divinity students begin preaching before graduation. Alexander was invited before he had finished his course of study to take Portland Chapel, Southampton, for three months, and the three months became twelve years. In the "Registry" of his preaching engagements which he kept for nearly sixty years, he dated the beginning of his Southampton pastorate June 28, 1846. His morning text on the epochal Sunday was "Fellow helpers to the truth" (III John 8). His evening text was, "I take you to record this day that I am free from the blood of all men and have not shunned to declare unto you all the counsel of God" (Acts 20:26). Within these spacious frontiers, his ministry thereafter was to be contained.

The date is significant not only for the beginning of Maclaren's ministry but for the agitations which then literally shook the Established Church in England to its foundations. A new social, industrial and political world was taking form through militant confusions. "There are," Carlyle had written, "great outward changes in progress," though he was confident that the planet would still be guarded by "deep Heaven." John Henry Newman and his friends were not entirely willing to trust the Established Church to "deep Heaven" without their guiding co-operation. The results had been the Tractarian Movement, clerical alarums and excursions, and finally Newman's submission to Rome, which had taken place eight months before Alexander Maclaren preached his first sermon at Southampton. John Morley thought Newman's act an "earthquake." Gladstone thought its calamitous importance could not be overestimated.

Nothing of all this disturbed the peace of Portland Chapel, and

---

[2] In general, he signed himself McLaren, but penciled under or over the signature Maclaren. The "McL" he thought looked ugly in print. The *Manchester Guardian* always printed "McLaren."

indeed why should it? In the vast and austere range of Calvinistic theology, John Henry Newman's submission to Rome was only a detail. During almost the entire period of Maclaren's ministry, the Free Churches were constantly striving to get themselves free from the disparities under which by the laws of England and the rather unfraternal dispositions of the Established Church they lived and moved and had their being. Mr. Matthew Arnold would soon be writing them down for their lack of culture, though the doors of the historic universities from which, according to Mr. Arnold, they might have absorbed a perfect culture were barred against them. Later, though this is to anticipate, Manchester would be a center and stronghold of political liberalism.

Surprisingly little of this either colored or informed Maclaren's preaching. Political and social agitation was not his vocation. Few of the outstanding preachers of the period were so apparently detached as Maclaren from the stormy currents of political and religious controversy. This is the more curious because his father-in-law was an "advanced liberal." Alexander loved beauty and the now vanished quiet of Southampton, which was far from being the port of entry then that it has become—scene of liners from the Seven Seas and the warships which protect them. Its countryside was particularly lovely and the "New Forest," already centuries old, was easily accessible. The not too distant Isle of Wight could be seen against the Solent and the genial climate was kind to a Scotchman nurtured in the north. Maclaren's delight in the beauty of nature was lifelong. Many of his most telling illustrations are drawn from nature, and there is throughout all his sermons a beautiful interweaving of the physical and spiritual worlds.

He had hardly begun to preach in Portland Chapel before it was full. He was much in demand for lecturing, one of the then popular diversions of the relatively unworldly. In the main he refused to be too much drawn upon by outside invitations and kept to his sermons and parish duties. He so laid the foundations upon which he afterwards built so spaciously. A photograph taken at Southampton when he was about thirty shows a face of classical regularity, deep-set eyes, broad forehead and rather delicate mouth. He is still entirely smooth-shaven and with abundant hair. He was described generally as slender. A snapshot taken years later makes him over average height. The Southampton photograph is rather earnestly self-conscious—a most promising young minister living up to the part.

Alexander married his cousin, Marian McLaren, in 1856. It was the happiest of marriages. Maclaren, among other things, was thus related through his mother-in-law to the Gifford family, to one of whom erudition owes the long succession of "Gifford Lectures." Sir Walter Raleigh, brilliant professor of English literature at Oxford, would have been a nephew of Lord Gifford and so a cousin, one suspects, in some degree of removal of Dr. Maclaren's. It was a marriage made in heaven, and Maclaren might have said of his wife as Tennyson said of his, "The peace of God came into my heart at the altar where I married her," though there would have been no altar in a Baptist marriage, but for all that the sacrament of love. "There has never been," he wrote after her death in 1884, "a cloud between us, and she never did a thing or spoke a word that was not full of love and unselfishness." Her pictures toward middle age show the serenest of faces framed by graying hair. They had three children, two daughters and a son.

Maclaren laid the foundations of his Manchester ministry in Southampton. His parishioners there thought his sermons to them the best he ever preached. His Southampton ministry fell into a quiet routine for which he was afterwards always thankful: two sermons of a Sunday, Monday Prayer Meeting, a Thursday service and lecture. The faultless beauty of his diction was already recognized. Though he won recognition outside Southampton slowly, it was bound to come. Union Chapel, Manchester, called him to be the pastor of the congregation there, in April, 1858. He accepted with reluctance, but the time was ripe for him to move. Thereafter he became "Maclaren of Manchester," known throughout Christendom.

The content and drama of the long Manchester years were in his preaching and his writing. Naturally his church prospered, and in time his congregation built him a new church of great beauty and dignity. The University of Edinburgh made him a doctor of divinity. Glasgow later gave him the same degree, and there was also from some institution I cannot specify, a degree in "Humane Letters." No ministry could have been happier. It was attended by foreign travel, once as far as Australia. Naturally he received denominational recognition, the highest his denomination could bestow, the presidency of the Baptist Union. All this together constituted a sequence of honor and accomplishment. His renown as a preacher grew coterminal with the English-speaking world and the crescent years did no more than whiten his hair and touch his face with benignity. Sir George Reid painted his portrait for the Manchester Art Gallery. This is by far the best of the extant photographs and portraits. The pose is exceedingly good and the canvas is washed with a mellow dignity. He wore no "bands" nor gown nor any clerical collar.

He did eventually substitute for that peculiar clerical insignia a white fringe of whiskers under his chin from ear to ear, the reason for which his biographers do not explain. It could hardly have been for adornment.

The way of a nonconformist minister in Maclaren's Great Britain was patterned, but not too rigorously. Tobacco was permitted and Maclaren took abstemious advantage of that permission. At least he said he did not smoke too much. The theater was not permitted, though possibly the music hall was. The Free Churches honored their ministers and were not too demanding save as to the sermon, for preaching had a consideration with them which their situations tended to enhance. Their services, being entirely nonliturgical, had only two supports, the devotion of the congregation, the leadership of the minister. When these were perfectly attuned, the result was a type of service as significant in quality as it was simple in form and rich in mystic power.

The devout silence of a British congregation in the twilight of its evening service is a spiritual wonder and a grace apart. It needs no pulse beat of liturgy to give it life, being life itself fed from deep internal forces. It receives the sermon with a sigh of expectation and has a power to lift even the most halting preacher from any low entanglement. The proud order of the Established Church in Maclaren's England refused the Free Church minister any parity of status or any recognition of sacramental authority; which was, save for what it did to the Established Church itself, the most inconsequential of intolerances. There was then as now another succession than a chain of Bishops—with possible missing links—and another ordination than the mitred could bestow.

Alexander Maclaren fitted perfectly into the Free Church order, and his pulpit became a throne. The detail of his long years in Manchester does not greatly matter, for there was across all the years a sustaining constancy. One shadow that fell across these years was the too early death of his wife, which left him a haunting loneliness. Time was kind to him and won him honor and recognition. The beauty of his chapel was arresting. He became a recognized part of the life of the great city. He was, as has been said, twice elected president of the Baptist Union, the highest honor the Baptists could pay him. His mission to Australia, already noted, was in 1883, and so on and on. He resigned as active pastor of Union Chapel in 1903. He had been pastor there for forty-five years. Four years later the congregation noted with deep interest that July 5, 1908, was the fiftieth anniversary of the commencement of his "ministerial work," whereupon they celebrated his semicentennial and passed fitting resolutions. He wrote in reply, "I can never be grateful enough for all the love, the forebearance, the help and inspiration I have received from the church and congregation of Union Chapel." He died in 1910 and was cremated. The cross above his ashes bears an inscription he himself had chosen, *"In Christo, in pace, in spe."*

Maclaren's sermons and Biblical expositions were and continue to be the deposit of his genius and his labor. The distinction between them is nominal. The sermons were basically expository; the expositions were in substance sermons. As this is being written, there are no available records of his occasional addresses, except before the meetings of the Baptist Union and these not in full. First and last he said or wrote a good deal about his preaching technique, though he does not seem ever to have made a book about preaching. In this too he was unique, for most of the outstanding preachers of his generation did at least one book on preaching. He was approached about giving a series of lectures at Yale on the Lyman Beecher foundation. He either declined or discouraged the invitation—a loss to the foundation and to all lovers of sound homiletic instruction.

He was controlled by his vocation and his vocation was controlled by his Christian devotion. In a sentence or two of obscure context, he had, he said, abjured "intellectual preaching"—by which he must have meant philosophical or even excessively theological preaching. His philosophy and his theology are always implicit rather than explicit in his sermons. He seems as preacher and expositor to have moved in a region unaffected by doctrinal controversy, or much more to the point, by Old and New Testament criticism, for one remembers that during all the latter part of his ministry questions of the authorship, composition, dating and authority, especially of the Old Testament, were burning and divisive questions. His serene aloofness from it all is outstanding and probably one of the secrets of his popular power. He accepted the Biblical records, based his sermons thereupon, but in general through analogy and vital interpretation he carried his texts into regions beyond controversy. There is an obscure reference to a time in which his orthodoxy was questioned, but why and by whom is not on the record.

"I have tried," he said to a company of ministers, "to preach Jesus Christ and the Jesus Christ not of the Gospels only, but the Christ of the Gospels and the Epistles. He is the source . . ." St. Paul said much the same thing of his own ministry: "Jesus Christ and him crucified . . ." Dr. Maclaren would have assented to another Pauline phrase, "My life is hid with Christ in God." That assent went deep, and as near as may be was the secret of his passion and his power. This he urged upon his congregation as the secret of any life victorious over temptation, sorrow and death.

It is right to say then that his preaching was Christ-centered. It was interpenetrated by inherited Protestant evangelism, a religious force as difficult precisely to define as it has been creatively potent. Throughout the range of his sermons he describes and designates, ceaselessly, distinctive qualities of a Christian life. It must begin in repentance, for which the sinner always had abundant need, for the sense of sin is strong in Maclaren's preaching, not so much specified sins of omission and commission as a fundamental gone-wrongness of human nature. Once saved by grace, the Christian had thereafter guidance, if so be he sought it, for all his pilgrim ways, strength enough for his burdens, wisdom for his perplexities, compensation for his losses and comfort for his sorrows. It is always a direct dealing with God through the mediation of Jesus Christ. Then the seeker may always know God's will and be sure of his nearness. When the soul thirsts after God enough, it is immediately satisfied.

"In the realm of communion with God, to desire is to have." Thereafter, in the contact of the seeking soul with God, there are rest and strength and fullness of life.

Maclaren's preaching, so centered, had a long, long radius. It included the whole of life's quests and experiences and touched the eternal. "Surely in our fleeting days the one means of securing for ourselves blessedness, rest and strength . . . is to knit ourselves to him who lives forever and whose love is as lasting as is life."

The needs and experiences to which Maclaren addressed himself and his all-sufficient Gospel were the needs and experiences of sinners wanting to be Christians and Christians wanting to be good Christians bravely meeting their trials, realizing all the possibilities and proving faithful to the end. The sins he indicts are the lapses of the individual. The goodness he urges is an individual goodness. He does not often pass outside the circumference of a life so circumscribed.

If he does preach any approximation to the social Gospel his preaching is conformed to these ruling ideas. Social rightness is only the projection of individual rightness. If Christians did not fight, there would be no war; if Christians were just, there would be no social injustice. All this to our minds, strongly under the influence of economic urges and group psychologies, would seem too simple.

There is no patterned rigidity in Maclaren's preaching, save possibly his habit of organizing his sermons under three sermonic heads. A plain-spoken critic once said that he served, so to speak, the bread of life with a three-pronged fork. Maclaren answered that for the most part that was the best way of organizing his sermons. He develops his motifs like a musician and evokes a rich variety from the major chords he is always striking, and all this for more than fifty years. There are twenty published volumes of his sermons, and they total 427 printed sermons. I do not know whether or not any other preacher has published so voluminously.

He was, as the phrase is commonly used, an "extemporary" preacher, though in his case that shopworn phrase is entirely misleading. It comes to this, that he did not use a manuscript nor memorize his sermons nor commonly write them, but they were for all that most carefully prepared, given thought form in the study and the garmenture of words in the pulpit. He secured always an immediacy of relation between preparation and delivery. "I must give it red hot," he said. He used condensed notes on which he was not greatly dependent and which like Robertson he often ignored. He was accustomed to write a few introductory sentences, as he said, to get going, and perhaps a conclusion. The first volume of sermons was based on stenographic reports—also his later volumes. The published prayers were taken entirely from stenographic reports and are of classic beauty of diction. Since for years his sermons were published in the *Manchester Guardian* the morning after their delivery, they must have somehow got written, possibly after delivery and before publication. Biographical sources are here somewhat indefinite. He is said to have made little changes in the stenographic reports before publication.

The most remarkable of Alexander Maclaren's gifts—or if you please, disciplined capacities—was his power of almost perfect "spoken composition." It was noted that he was one of the few preachers who spoke better than he wrote. These sermons whose stenographic reports needed and received so little correction read as if they had been written with the utmost care. Their forms are balanced; words are chosen with astounding felicity. There are always mystic gleams and exquisite analogies drawn from nature. I should think Maclaren's facility in this most difficult of all arts, to create literature in the very act of delivery, to have been then and still unmatched. His face was said in its mobility of expressions to have enthralled those who watched him. His voice was equal to any occasion. It is noted how one great audience straining to hear in a hall of acoustical bewilderment welcomed at last a preacher who could be heard. His Scotch accent gave its tempo to what he said and particularly the structural support of its stress upon the consonants and its burred r's.

All of these endowments and achievements seem to me even less remarkable than Maclaren's primacy as an expository and textual preacher. The preaching was Biblically based and vitally directed. His texts, his topics, and his organization are always in a mutually supporting harmony. For a preacher may be expository, textual, topical, or a mixture of them all. If he be an expository preacher, he has for guidance the contours of the passages. If he be textual, he has the content of the text for what the medieval experts in homiletics called dilation. If he be topical, he has his topic. But if he combine the textual and the topical and make the text primary, then the topic must have been implicit or explicit in the text. What is called homiletic genius is the faculty of discovering the unexpected in a perhaps shopworn text, with an entire honesty in dealing with the text itself. All this one supposes is due to the preacher's association lines. The text leads one man in one direction and another in a quite different direction. Now Maclaren possessed a gift unmatched in sermonic literature, the gift to evoke from the text a topic of force or beauty or suggestion so entirely consistent with the text itself that thereafter both text and topic sing together for joy there made. If and as the text goes in one direction and the topic in another, the result is distressing. With Maclaren the text and topic always go in the same direction, mounting up with wings as eagles. He needed no homiletic gymnastics to keep them in chain.

I do not know which came first, though I suspect the text, but the topic is never imposed: it burgeons, so to speak, out of the text. The topic, of course, may be textually specific—"Phillip the Evangelist" or "Simeon's Swan Song" or "Jesus Christ Charged with Blasphemy" or "Salted with Fire." In other instances the topic, while always there, is Maclaren's own discovery and vision. Any careful comparison in the long list of his sermons of the text and the topics would be at once a sound homiletic discipline and a temptation to borrow from so boundless a wealth.

In perhaps the majority of his sermons Maclaren is the expositor in the pulpit, but in another dimension he is the poet and the seer, with the guiding light without which preaching perishes. The account of the king of Israel who claimed as his own what the king of Syria held yields the topic "Unpossessed Possessions"—and the sermon thereafter preaches itself. Any preacher will still be fascinated by the wisdom and allure of his topics and occasionally their almost inspired gleams.

His bases are always Biblical. Often he follows through a book or a religious series of episodés. He was at home equally in both Testaments. Out of 49 sermons in *Leaves from the Tree of Life,* 24 are from the New Testament, 25 from the Old, and the Old Testament sermons for imagination and sublimate poetry are the better. He quoted sparingly, Browning a little, Tennyson more often, for he was contemporary with "In Memoriam." His illustrations are mostly Biblical or else from nature, sensitively seized and often beautifully phrased. There is little use of contemporaneous literature or much history outside the Bible. He repeats of course; even the most opulent of preachers has his limits, but his development of the same text is never twice the same. His organization, as has been said, is predominantly three point, and his faculty for getting these three points out of his text are part of the free course of his thought, his homiletic genius, and for the most part unexpectedly simple and direct. For example, "Concerning the Crown": I. The crown, II. The discipline by which the crown is won, III. The power of the reward as motive for life.

Maclaren's technique has made him outstandingly the preachers' preacher. Published volumes of his sermons contain pages of testimony as to Maclaren's predominant station. This accounts in part, one suspects, for the continuing demand for his published sermons. They are almost fatally easy for another preacher to adapt for his own ends, and there must for years have been echoes of them wherever the English language was spoken. (An appendix to *Leaves from the Tree of Life* cites such laudatory tributes from outstanding preachers of the last generation as I suppose no other preacher received.) Perhaps more wisely used than merely to repreach them, they do illustrate the always unexhausted of Biblical preaching and the response it always wins, if rightly done, from the congregation. For that alone, Maclaren's sermons still merit the careful study of any preacher.

In the main, his introductions are either expository or exegetical, that is, they "place" the text or its wording. He makes much of nuances and overtones of translation, and very often supplies translations of his own, for Greek and Hebrew were also his mother tongues. He had, as noted, a gift for novel organization of familiar texts. For example, "The Two Paths"—"Enter ye in at the strait gate . . ." etc. There is an expository introduction; then I. The gates, II. The roads contrasted, III. Note the travelers, and IV. The contrasted ends of the two paths. There are heights of oratorical passion Maclaren never reaches. His constant elevation is his power. He does not excel in oratorical perorations and is more likely to end as he began with his text. The sermons for the most part are relatively short, some of them unexpectedly short. He lacks the massiveness of development of which Channing, for example, was capable, the constant interplay of analogy which distinguishes Martineau, and so on in comparison. His gifts were distinctly his own.

The Epositor's Bible series took form and content during his ministry. Naturally he was called upon to contribute. Again in the main his expositions are substantially homiletic, meant for a preacher's use and so abundantly used unstintingly. All the old Expositor's Bible volumes were gold mines for a young preacher, and most of us of a now vanishing generation lined our bare book shelves with them. Nor do I know that anything since has taken their place. Maclaren wrote comments on the International Sunday School lessons for the *American Times* for twenty years. This alone would guarantee his unimpeachable orthodoxy, or else some canny combination of the wisdom of the serpent with the harmlessness of the dove. He called his weekly contributions "The Yankees." His letters reveal his concern for getting them done and started across the Atlantic in season, no slight accomplishment. This connection made him well-known in America and brought appeals to come to America for preaching and lecturing. As noted he was asked to deliver the Yale lectures, and Dale entreated him to accept. He regretted, he said, never to have seen Amrica, but though he might go down under to Australia, he never crossed the Atlantic. Toward the end, he habituated himself to the use of the typewriter, and no machine could have been more constantly or creatively or opulently employed, for the content of what he did still in print is really very great.

He should, of course, in a more extended study be compared with his contemporaries in the pulpits of the Free and Established Churches far beyond the comparisons here made, for his homiletic contemporaries were a stellar group, and few stars of equal magnitude have since taken their place. It is significant that he and Martineau were good friends, though almost poles apart in their theological attitudes. Their kinship was the kinship of two poet preachers, for each was a master of the written or spoken word.

Robertson Nicoll, whose judgments made or unmade preachers, said of Maclaren (for this study to end with):

"From his youth he looked like a Highland chieftain, born to command. Before you knew he was a prophet you were sure he was a king. Who can forget that wonderful face, tender and stern, more beautiful and saintly

as the years went on, with the lights and shadows sweeping over it. . . .
In the pulpit . . . you could see the double process going on—the mind
shaping the consummate sentence behind the act and ardor of utterance.
. . . He commanded words as an emperor and as a magician. In his
loftiest flights one hardly knew whether he spake or sang. It was "spirit
half asleep or song half awake!"

This volume undertakes to recapture in its compilation of Maclaren's
sermons what can be recaptured from music when the singer is gone.
Each sermon is preceded by a meditation and followed by a prayer.
The editor has attempted wherever possible to obtain unity in the
meditations and prayers.

Gaius Glenn Atkins

The Best of
ALEXANDER MACLAREN

THE COMPLETE LIFE [1]

Scaffoldings are for buildings, and the moments and days and years of our earthly lives are scaffolding. What are you building inside the scaffolding, brother? What kind of a structure will be disclosed when the scaffolding is knocked away? What is the end for which days and years are given? That they may give us what eternity cannot take away —a character built upon the love of God in Christ, and molded into His likeness. "Man's chief end is to glorify God and to enjoy Him for ever." Has your life helped you do that? If it has, though you be but a child, you are full of years; if it has not, though your hair be whitened with the snows of the nineties, you are yet incomplete and immature. The great end of life is to make us like Christ, and pleasing to Christ. If life has done that for us we have got the best out of it, and our life is completed, whatever may be the number of the days. Quality, not quantity, is the thing that determines the perfectness of a life.

[1] From *Similes and Figures from Alexander Maclaren*, by Francis E. Clark. Copyright, 1910, by Fleming H. Revell, and reprinted by permission.

1. THE MEASURE OF IMMEASURABLE POWER [1]

"That ye may know . . . what is the exceeding greatness of his power to usward who believe, according to the working of his mighty power, which he wrought in Christ." EPH. 1:19, 20.

"The riches of the glory of the inheritance" will sometimes quench rather than stimulate hope. He can have little depth of religion who has not often felt that the transcendent glory of that promised future sharpens the doubt—"and can *I* ever hope to reach it?" Our paths are strewn with battlefields where we were defeated; how should we expect the victor's wreath? And so Paul does not think that he has asked all which his friends in Ephesus need when he has asked that they may know the hope and the inheritance. There is something more wanted, something more even for our knowledge of these, and that is the knowledge of the power which alone can fulfill the hope and bring the inheritance. His language swells and peals and becomes exuberant and noble with his theme. He catches fire, as it were, as he thinks about this power that worketh in us. It is "exceeding." Exceeding what? He does not tell us, but other words in this letter, in the other great prayer which it contains, may help us to supply the missing words. He speaks of the "love of Christ which passeth knowledge," and of God being "able to do exceedingly abundantly above all that we can ask or think." The power which is really at work in Christian men today is in its nature properly transcendent and immeasurable, and passes thought and desire and knowledge.

And yet it has a measure. "According to the working of the strength of the might which he wrought in Christ." Is that heaping together of synonyms, or all but synonyms, mere tautology? Surely not. Commentators tell us that they can distinguish differences of meaning between

---
[1] From *The God of the Amen,* Alexander & Shepheard (London), 1891.

the words, in that the first of them is the more active and outward, and the last of them is the more inward. And so we liken them to fruit and branch and root: but we need simply say that the gathering together of words so nearly co-extensive in their meaning is witness to the effort to condense the infinite within the bounds of human tongue, to speak the unspeakable; and that these reiterated expressions, like the blows of the billows that succeed one another on the beach, are hints of the force of the infinite ocean that lies behind.

And then the Apostle, when he has once come in sight of his risen Lord, as is His wont, is swept away by the ardor of his faith and the clearness of his vision, and breaks from his purpose to dilate on the glories of his King. We do not need to follow him into that. I limit myself this morning to the words which I have read as my text, with only such reference to the magnificent passage which succeeds as may be necessary for the exposition of this.

I. So, then, I ask you to look, first, at the measure and example of the immeasurable power that works in Christian men.

"According to the working of the strength of the might which he wrought in Christ." The Resurrection, the Ascension, the session at the right hand of God, the rule over all creatures, and the exaltation above all things on earth or in the heavens—these are the things which the Apostle brings before us as the pattern-works, the *chef-d'oeuvre* of the power that is operating in all Christians. The present glories of the ascended Christ are glories possessed by a man, and, that being so, they are available as evidences and measures of the power which works in believing souls. In them we see the possibilities of humanity, the ideal for man which God had when He created and breathed His blessing upon him. It is one of ourselves who has strength enough to bear the burden of the glory, one of ourselves who can stand within the blaze of encircling and indwelling Divinity and be unconsumed. The possibilities of human nature are manifest there. If we want to know what the Divine power can make of us, let us turn to look with the eye of faith upon what it has made of Jesus Christ.

But such a thought, glorious as it is, still leaves room for doubt as to my personal attainment of such an ideal. Possibility is much, but we need solid certainty. And we find it in the truth that the bond between Christ and those who truly love and trust Him is such as that the possibility must become a reality and be consolidated into a certainty. The Vine and its branches, the members and their Head, the Christ and His Church, are knit together by such closeness of union as that wheresoever and whatsoever the one is, there, and that, must the others also be.

Therefore, when doubts and fears, and consciousness of my own weakness, creep across me, and all my hopes are dimmed, as some star in the heavens is, when a light mist floats between us and it, let us turn away to Him our brother, bone of our bone and flesh of our flesh, and think that He, in His calm exaltation and regal authority and infinite blessedness, is not only the pattern of what humanity may be, but the pledge of what His Church must be. "The glory that thou gavest me I have given them."

Nor is that all. Not only a possibility and a certainty for the future are for us the measure of the power that worketh in us, but as this same letter teaches us, we have as Christians, a present scale by which we may estimate the greatness of the power. For in the next chapter, after that glorious burst as to the dignity of His Lord, which we have not the heart to call a digression, the Apostle, recurring to the theme of my text, goes on to say, "And you hath he quickened." And then, catching it up a verse or two afterwards, reiterates, clause by clause, what had been done on Jesus as having been done on us Christians. If that Divine Spirit raised Him from the dead, and set Him at His own right hand in the heavenly places, it is as true that the same power hath "raised us up together, and made us sit together in heavenly places in Christ Jesus." And so not only the far-off, though real and brilliant, and eye and heart-filling glories of the ascended Christ give us the measure of the power, but also the limited experience of the present Christian life, the fact of the resurrection from the true death, the death of sin, the fact of union with Jesus Christ so real and close as that they who truly experience it do live, as far as the roots of their lives are concerned, and the scope and the aim of them, "in the heavens," and "sit with him in heavenly places"—these things afford us the measure of the power that worketh in us.

Then, because a Man is King of kings and Lord of lords; and because He who is our Life "is exalted high above all principalities and powers"; and because from His throne He has quickened us from the death of sin, and has drawn us so near to Himself that if we are His we truly live beside Him, even whilst we stumble here in the darkness, we may know the exceeding greatness of His power according to the working of the strength of the might which He wrought in Christ when He raised Him from the dead.

II. Secondly, notice the knowledge of the unknowable power.

We have already come across the same apparent paradox, covering a deep truth, in the former sections of this series of petitions. I need only remind you, in reference to this matter, that the knowledge which is here in question is not the intellectual perception of a fact as revealed in Scripture, but is that knowledge to which alone the New Testament gives the noble name, being knowledge verified by inward experience, and the result of one's own personal acquaintance with its object.

How do we know a power? By thrilling beneath its force. How are we to know the greatness of the power but because it comes surging and rejoicing into our aching emptiness, and lifts us buoyant above our temptations and weakness? Paul was not asking for these people theological conceptions. He was asking that their spirits might be so saturated with and immersed in that great ocean of force that pours from God as that they should never, henceforth, be able to doubt the greatness of that power which works in them. The knowledge that comes from experience is the knowledge that we all ought to seek. It is not merely to be desired that we should have right and just conceptions, but that we should have the vital knowledge which is, and which comes from, life eternal.

And that power, which thus we may all know by feeling it working upon ourselves, though it be immeasurable, has its measure; though it be, in its depth and fullness, unknowable and inexhaustible, may yet be really and truly known. You do not need a thunderstorm to experience the electric shock; a battery that you can carry in your pocket will do that for you. You do not need to have traversed all the length and breadth and depth and height of some newly-discovered country to be sure of its existence, and to have a real, though it may be a vague, conception of the magnitude of its shores. And so, really, though boundedly, we have the knowledge of God, and can rely upon it as valid, though partial; and similarly, by experience, we have such a certified acquaintance with Him and His power as needs no enlargement to be trusted, and to become the source of blessings untold. We may see but a strip of the sky through the narrow chinks of our prison windows, and many a grating may further intercept the view, and much dust that might be cleared away may dim the glass, but yet it *is* the sky that we see, and we can think of the great horizon circling round and round, and of the infinite depths above there, which neither eye nor thought can travel unwearied. Though all that we see be but an inch in breadth and a foot or two in height, yet we do see. We know the unknowable power that passeth knowledge.

And let me remind you of how large importance this knowledge of and constant reference to the measureless power manifested in Christ is for us. I believe there can be no vigorous, happy Christian life without it. It is our only refuge from pessimism and despair for the world. The old psalm said, "Thou hast crowned him with glory and honour, and hast given him dominion over the works of thy hands." And hundreds of years afterwards the writer of the Epistle to the Hebrews commented on it thus, "We see not yet all things put under him." Was the old vision a dream, was it never intended to be fulfilled? Apparently so, if we take the history of the past into account, and the centuries that have passed since have done nothing to make it more probable, apart from Jesus Christ, that man will rise to the heights which the psalmist dreamed of. When we look at the exploded Utopias that fill the past; when we think of the strange and apparently fatal necessity by which evil is developed from every stage of what men call progress, and how improvement is perverted, almost as soon as effected, into another fortress of weakness and misery; when we look on the world as it is today, I know not whence a man is to draw bright hopes, or what is to deliver him from pessimism as his last word about himself and his fellows, except the "working of the strength of the might which he wrought in Christ." "We see not yet all things put under him." Be it so, "but we see Jesus," and, looking to Him, hope is possible, reasonable, and imperative.

The same knowledge is our refuge from our own consciousness of weakness. We look up, as a climber may do in some Alpine ravine, upon the smooth gleaming walls of the cliff that rises above him. It is marble, it is fair, there are lovely lands on the summit, but nothing that has not wings can get there. We try but slip backwards almost as much as we rise. What is to be done? Are we to sit down at the foot of the cliff, and say, "We cannot climb, let us be content with the luscious herbage and sheltered ease below?" Yes! That is what we are tempted to say. But look! a mighty hand reaches over, an arm is stretched down, the hand grasps us, and lifts us, and sets us there.

"No man hath ascended up into heaven save he that came down from heaven," and having returned thither stoops thence, and will lift us to Himself. I am a poor, weak creature. Yes! I am all full of sin and corruption. Yes! I am ashamed of myself every day. Yes! I am too heavy to climb, and have no wings to fly, and am bound here by chains manifold. Yes! But we know the exceeding greatness of the power, and we triumph in Him.

That knowledge should shame us into contrition, when we think of such force at our disposal, and so poor results. That knowledge should widen our conceptions, enlarge our desires, breathe a brave confidence into our hopes, should teach us to expect great things of God, and to be intolerant of present attainments whilst anything remains unattained. And it should stimulate our vigorous effort, for no man will long seek to be better if he is convinced that the effort is hopeless.

Learn to realize the exceeding greatness of the power that will clothe your weakness. "Lift up your eyes on high, and behold who hath created these things, for that he is strong in might, not one faileth." That is wonderful, but here is a far nobler operation of the Divine power. It is great to preserve the ancient heavens fresh and strong by His might, but it is greater to come down to my weakness, to "give power to the faint," and to "increase strength to them that have no might." And that is what He will do with us.

III. Lastly, notice the conditions for the operations of the power.

"To usward who believe," says Paul. He has been talking to these Ephesians, and saying "Ye," but now, by that "us," he places himself beside them, identifies himself with them, and declares that all his gifts and strength come to him on precisely the same conditions on which theirs do to them; and that he, like them, is a waiter upon that grace which God bestows on them that trust Him.

"To usward who believe." Once more we are back at the old truth which we can never make too emphatic and plain, that the one condition of the weakest among us being strong with the strength of the Lord is simple trust in Him, verified, of course, by continuance and by effort.

How did the water go into the Ship Canal at Eastham last week? First of all they cut a trench, and then they severed the little strip of land between the hole and the sea, and the sea did the rest. The wider and deeper the opening that we make in our natures by our simple trust in God, the fuller will be the rejoicing flood that pours into us. There is an old story about a Christian father, who, having been torturing himself with theological speculations about the nature of the Trinity, fell asleep and dreamed that he was emptying the ocean with a thimble! Well, you cannot empty it with a thimble, but you can go to it with one, and, if you have only a thimble in your hand, you will only bring away a thimbleful. The measure of your faith is the measure of God's power given to you.

There are two measures of the immeasurable power; the one is that infinite limit of "the power which he wrought in Christ," and the other the practical limit. The working measure of our spiritual life is our faith. In plain English, we can have as much of God as we want. We do have as much as we want. And if, in touch with the power that can shatter a universe, we only get a little thrill that is scarcely perceptible to ourselves, and all unnoticed by others, whose fault is that? And if, coming to the fountain that laughs at drought, and can fill a universe with its waters, we scarcely bear away a straitened drop or two, that barely refreshes our parched lips, and does nothing to stimulate the growth of the plants of holiness in our gardens, whose fault is that? The practical measure of the power is for us the measure of our belief and desire. And if we only go to Him, as I pray we all may, and continue there, and ask from Him strength, according to the riches that are treasured in Jesus Christ, we shall get the old answer, "According to your faith be it unto you."

O Lord! Whose paths are all paths of peace, help us, we beseech Thee, though with faltering steps and slow, to tread in Christ's footsteps and take Him for our Leader and our Guide.

We thank Thee that we can bring all our weakness to Thyself in the assured confidence that Thy strength will be ours. Thou givest power to the faint, and "to them that have no might Thou dost increase strength." When we think of Thee as "fainting not, neither weary," may we ever feel that we have a portion in that great storehouse of undecaying and unexhausted power; and to us, and for us, may it be true that we shall be ready for all the great moments of life in which there are calls made on us for special effort, that we shall "run and not be weary"; and that in all the common moments of life, when the same small duties have to be done over and over again, our patience may hold out, and we "walk and not faint."

To these ends, O Lord, Help us, we beseech Thee, ever to "mount up with wings as eagles," and in aspiration towards Thyself, and set our affections and minds on things above. May we be raised above our own weaknesses, and possess that power on which time and decay have no force.

Hear us, we beseech Thee, in our prayer; mercifully accept and answer us, for our Saviour Christ's sake. Amen.[2]

---

[2] From *Pulpit Prayers*.

ALL THINGS ARE YOURS [1]

Everything is a friend to the man that loves God in a far sweeter and deeper sense than it can ever be to any other. Like a sudden burst of sunshine upon a gloomy landscape, the light of union with God and friendship with Him flooding my daily life flashes it all up into brightness. The dark ribbon of the river that went creeping through the black copses, when the sun glints upon it, gleams up into links of silver, and the trees by its bank blaze out into green and gold. Brethren, "who follows pleasure follows pain"; who follows God finds pleasure following Him.

There can be no surer way to set the world against me than to try to make it for me, and to make it my all. They tell us that if you want to count those stars that, "like a swarm of fireflies tangled in a silver braid," make up the Pleiades, the surest way to see the greatest number of them is to look a little on one side of them. Look away from the joys and friendships of creatural things, right up to God, and you will see these sparkling and dancing in the skies, as you never see them when you gaze at them alone. Make them second, and they are good and on your side. Make them first, and they will turn to be your enemies and fight against you.

[1] From *Similes and Figures from Alexander Maclaren,* by Francis E. Clark. Copyright, 1910, by Fleming H. Revell, and reprinted by permission.

2. GOD'S GUESTS [1]

"One thing have I desired of the Lord, that will I seek after; that I may dwell in the house of the Lord all the days of my life." Ps. 27:4.

We shall do great injustice to this mystical aspiration of the psalmist, if we degrade it to be the mere expression of a desire for unbroken residence in a material temple. He was no sickly, sentimental seeker after cloistered seclusion. He knew the necessities and duties of life far better than in a cowardly way to wish to shirk them, in order that he might loiter in the temple, idle, under the pretense of worship. Nor would the saying fit into the facts of the case if we gave it that low meaning, for no person had his residence in the temple. And what follows in the next verse would, on that hypothesis, be entirely inappropriate. "In the secret of his tabernacle shall he hide me." No one went "into the secret place of the Most High," in the visible, material structure, except the high priest once a year. But this singer expects that his abode will be there always; and that, in the time of trouble, he can find refuge there.

Apart altogether from any wider considerations as to the relation between form and spirit under the Old Covenant, I think that such observations compel us to see in these words a desire a great deal nobler and deeper than any such wish.

I. Let us, then, note the true meaning of this aspiration of the Psalmist's.

Its fulfillment depends not on where we are, but on what we think and feel; for every place is God's house, and what the psalmist desires is that he should be able to keep up unbroken consciousness of being in God's presence and should be always in touch with Him. That seems hard, and people say, "Impossible! how can I get above my daily work, and be perpetually thinking of God and His will, and consciously realiz-

---
[1] From *Triumphant Certainties,* American Baptist Publication Society, 1897.

ing communion with Him?" But there is such a thing as having an undercurrent of consciousness running all through a man's life and mind; such a thing as having a melody sounding in our ears perpetually, "so sweet we know not we are listening to it" until it stops and then, by the poverty of the naked and silent atmosphere, we know how musical were the sounds that we scarcely knew we heard, and yet did hear so well high above all the din of earth's noises.

Every man that has ever cherished such an aspiration as this knows the difficulties all too well. And yet, without entering upon thorny and unprofitable questions as to whether the absolute, unbroken continuity of consciousness of being in God's presence is possible for men here below, let us look at the question, which has a great deal more bearing upon our present condition—viz., whether a greater continuity of that consciousness is not possible than we attain to today. It does seem to me to be a foolish and miserable waste of time, and temper, and energy for good people to be quarreling about whether they can come to the absolute realization of this desire in this world, when there is not one of them that is not leagues below the possible realization of it, and knows that he is. At all events, whether or not the line can be drawn without a break at all, the breaks might be a great deal shorter and a great deal less frequent than they are. An unbroken line of conscious communion with God is the ideal; and that is what this singer desired and worked for. How many of my feelings and thoughts today, or of the things that I have said and done since I woke this morning, would have been done and said and felt exactly the same, if there were not a God at all, or if it did not matter in the least whether I ever came into touch with Him or not? Oh! dear friends, it is no vain effort to bring our lives a little nearer that unbroken continuity of communion with Him of which this text speaks. And God knows, and we each for ourselves know, how much and how sore our need is of such a union. "One thing have I desired, that will I seek after; that I"—in Mosley Street; I, in my study; I, in my shop; I, in my parlor, kitchen, or nursery; I, in my studio; I, in my lecture hall—"may dwell in the house of the Lord all the days of my life." In our "Father's house are many mansions." The room that we spend most of our lives in, each of us at our tasks or our work tables, may be in our Father's house, too; and it is only we that can secure that it shall be.

The inmost meaning of this psalmist's desire is that the consciousness of God shall be diffused throughout the whole of a man's days, instead of being coagulated here and there at points. The Australian rivers in a drought present a picture of the Christian life of far too many of us— a stagnant, stinking pool here, a stretch of blinding gravel there; another little drop of water a mile away, then a long line of foul-smelling mud, and then another shallow pond. Why! it ought to run in a clear stream, that has a scour in it, and that will take all filth off the surface.

The psalmist longed to break down the distinction between sacred and secular; to consecrate work, of whatsoever sort it was. He had learned what so many of us need to learn far more thoroughly, that if our religion does not drive the wheels of our daily business, it is of little use; and that if the field in which our religion has power to control and impel is not that of the trivialities and secularities of our ordinary life, there is no field for it at all.

"All the days of my life." Not only on Wednesday nights in this lecture room, while Tuesday and Thursday are given to the world and self; not only on Sundays; not for five minutes in the morning, when I am eager to get to my daily work, and less than five minutes at night, when I am half asleep, but through the long day, doing this, that, and the other thing for God and by God and with God, and making Him the motive and the power of my course, and my companion to heaven. And if we have, in our lives, things over which we cannot make the sign of the cross, the sooner we get rid of them the better; and if there is anything in our daily work, or in our characters, about which we are doubtful, here is a good test: does it seem to check our continual communion with God, as a ligature round the wrist might do the continual flow of the blood, or does it help us to realize His presence? If the former, let us have no more to do with it; if the latter, let us seek to increase it.

II. And now let me say a word about the psalmist's reason for this aspiration.

The word which he employs carries with it a picture, which is even more vividly given us by a synonymous word employed in the same connection in some of the other psalms. "That I may dwell in the house of the Lord"—now, that is an allusion, not only, as I think, to the temple, but also to the Oriental habit of giving a man, who took refuge in the tent of the sheikh, guest-rites of protection and provision and friendship. The habit exists to this day, and travelers among the Bedouins tell us lovely stories of how even an enemy with the blood of the closest relative of the owner of the tent on his hands, if he can once get in there and partake of the salt of the host, is safe, and the first obligation of the owner of the tent is to watch over the life of the fugitive as over his own.

So the psalmist says, "I desire to have guest-rites in thy tent; to lift up its folds, and shelter there from the heat of the desert. And although I be dark and stained with many evils and transgressions against thee, yet I come to claim the hospitality and provision and protection and friendship which the laws of the house do bestow upon a guest." Carrying out substantially the same idea, Paul tells the Ephesians, as if it were the very highest privilege that the Gospel brought to the Gentiles: "Ye are no more strangers, but fellow-citizens with the saints, and *of the household of God*"; incorporated into His family, and dwelling safely in His pavilion as their home.

That is to say, the blessedness of keeping up such a continual consciousness of touch with God is, first and foremost, the certainty of infallible protection. Oh! how it minimizes all trouble and brightens all joys, and calms amidst all distractions, and steadies and sobers in all circumstances, to feel ever the hand of God upon us! He who goes through life, finding that, when he has trouble to meet, it throws him back on God, and that, when bright mornings of joy drive away nights of weeping, these wake morning songs of praise, and are brightest because they shine with the light of a Father's love, will never be unduly moved by any vicissitudes of fortune. Like some inland and sheltered valley, with great mountains shutting it in, that "heareth not the loud winds when they call" beyond the barriers that enclose it, our lives may be tranquilly free from distraction, and may be full of peace, of nobleness, and of strength, on condition of our keeping in God's house all the days of our lives.

There is another blessing that will come to the dweller in God's house, and not a small one. It is that, by the power of this one satisfied longing, driven like an iron rod through all the tortuosities of my life, there will come into it a unity which otherwise few lives are ever able to attain, and the want of which is no small cause of the misery that is great upon men. Most of us seem, to our own consciousness, to live amidst endless distractions all our days, and our lives to be a heap of links parted from each other rather than a chain. But if we have that one constant thought with us, and if we are, through all the variety of occupations, true to the one purpose of serving and keeping near God, then we have a charm against the frittering away of our lives in distractions, and the misery of multiplicity; and we enter into the blessedness of unity and singleness of purpose; and our lives become, like the starry heavens in all the variety of their motions, obedient to one impulse. For unity in a life does not depend upon the monotony of its tasks, but upon the simplicity of the motive which impels to all varieties of work. So it is possible for a man harassed by multitudinous avocations, and drawn hither and thither by sometimes apparently conflicting and always bewildering, rapidly-following duties, to say, "This one thing I do," if all his doings are equally acts of obedience to God.

III. So, lastly, note the method by which this desire is realized. "One thing have I desired . . . that will I seek after." There are two points to be kept in view to that end. A great many people say, "One thing have I desired," and fail in persistent continuousness of the desire. No man gets rights of residence in God's house for a longer time than he continues to seek for them. The most advanced of us, and those that have longest been like Anna, who "departed not from the temple" day nor night, will certainly eject ourselves unless, like the psalmist, we use the verbs in both tenses, and say, "One thing *have* I desired . . . that *will* I seek after." John Bunyan saw that there was a back door to the lower regions close by the gates of the Celestial City. There may be men who have long lived beneath the shadow of the sanctuary, and at the last shall be found outside the gates.

But the words of the text not only suggest, by the two tenses of the verbs, the continuity of the desire which is destined to be granted, but also by the two verbs themselves—desire and seek after—the necessity of uniting prayer and work. Many desires are unsatisfied because conduct does not correspond to desires. Many a prayer for greater holiness and closer communion with God remains unanswered because its pray-ers never do anything to fulfill their prayers. I do not say they are hypocrites; certainly they are not consciously so, but I do say that there is a large measure of conventionality that means nothing, in the prayers of average Christian people for more holiness and likeness to Jesus Christ.

Dear friends, if we want this desire of dwelling in the house of the Lord to be fulfilled, the day's work must run in the same direction as the morning's petition, and we must, like the psalmist, say, "I *have desired* it of the Lord, and I, for my part, *will seek after it.*" Then, whether or not we reach absolutely to the standard, which is none the less to be aimed at, though it seems beyond reach, we shall draw nearer and nearer to it; and, God helping our weakness and increasing our strength, quickening us to "desire," and upholding us to "seek after," we may hope that, when the days of our life are past, we shall but remove into an upper chamber, more open to the sunrise and flooded with light; and shall go no more out, but "dwell in the house of the Lord forever."

O Lord, our gracious Father! We beseech Thee to help us to draw near to Thee in our hour of prayer. We know that we bring with us much that hinders our souls' desires rising to Thyself; duties which Thou dost lay upon us; the cares which are inseparable from our earthly condition. But we beseech Thee that Thou wouldst help us now to deliver our hearts from the bonds that sometimes hold them, and that Thou wouldst open our eyes to behold the things that are, though we so often lose sight of them amidst the things that seem to be.

We thank Thee for the opportunity of assembling together and seeking Thy face. We thank Thee for all the circumstances and mercies of another day. We beseech Thee that now we may each be able, and the more able because we are gathered together, to draw near to Thee. We thank Thee that Thou dost approach and answer the solitary petitions of Thy scattered servants. We bless Thee that Thou dost draw near to them when, with one accord, they lift up their voices in supplication to Thee; and we pray Thee that our services may never be without the demonstration of the Spirit and of power, and that we may all feel that in very deed it is no vain thing to wait upon God.

All we ask is for Christ our Saviour's sake. Amen.[2]

---
[2] From *Pulpit Prayers*.

STRENGTHENED WITH MIGHT [1]

There is no part of my being that is not patent to the tread of this Divine Guest. There are no rooms of the house of my spirit, into which He may not go. Let Him come with the master key in His hand into all the dim chambers of your feeble nature; and as the one life is light in the eye, and color in the cheek, and deftness in the fingers, and strength in the arm, and pulsation in the heart, so He will come with the manifold results of the one gift to you. He will be like some subtle elixir which, taken into the lips, steals through a pallid and wasted frame, and brings back a glow to the cheek and a luster to the eye, and swiftness to the brain, and power to the whole nature. Or as some plant, drooping and flagging beneath the hot rays of the sun, when it has the scent of water given to it, will, in all its parts, stiffen and erect itself, so when the Spirit is poured out on men, their whole nature is invigorated and helped.

[1] From *Similes and Figures from Alexander Maclaren,* by Francis E. Clark. Copyright, 1910, by Fleming H. Revell, and reprinted by permission.

3. UNPOSSESSED POSSESSIONS [1]

"And the King of Israel said unto his servants, Know ye that Ramoth in Gilead is ours, and we be still, and take it not out of the hand of the King of Syria?" I KINGS 22:3.

This city of Ramoth in Gilead was an important fortified place on the eastern side of the Jordan, and had, many years before our text, been captured by the northern neighbors in the kingdom of Syria. A treaty had subsequently been concluded and broken, a war followed thereafter, in which Benhadad, king of Syria, had bound himself to restore all his conquests. He had not observed that article of peace, and the people of Israel had not been strong enough to enforce it until the date of our text; but then, backed up by a powerful alliance with Jehoshaphat of Judah, they determined to make a dash to get back what was theirs, but whilst theirs was also not theirs.

Now, I have nothing more to do with Ahab and Jehoshaphat, but I want to turn the words of my text, and the thoughts that may come from them, into a direction profitable to ourselves. "Know ye that Ramoth in Gilead is ours?" and yet it had to be got out of the hands of the King of Syria.

I. What is ours and not ours.

Every Christian man has large tracts of unannexed territory, unattained possibilities, unenjoyed blessings, things that are his and yet not his. How much more of God you and I have a right to than we have the possession of! The ocean is ours, but only the little pailful that we carry away home to our own houses is of use to us. The whole of God is mine if I am Christ's, and a dribble of God is all that comes into the lives of most of us.

How much inward peace is ours! It is meant that there should never

---
[1] From *Christ's Musts*, Hodder & Stoughton Ltd. (London). Reprinted by permission.

pass across a Christian's soul more than a ripple of agitation, which may indeed ruffle and curl the surface; but deep down there should be the tranquillity of the fathomless ocean, unbroken by any tempests, and yet not stagnant, because there is a vital current that runs through it, and every drop is being drawn upward to the surface and the sunlight. There may be a peace in our hearts deep as life; a tranquillity which may be superficially disturbed, but is never thoroughly, and down to the depths, broken. And yet, let some little petty annoyance come into my daily life, and what a pucker I am in! Then we forget all about the still depths that we ought to be living in; and fears and hopes and loves and ambitions disturb our souls, just as they do the spirits of the men that do not profess to have any holdfast in God. The peace of God is ours; but, ah! in how sad a sense it is true that the peace of God is *not* ours!

What "heights"—for Ramoth means "high places"—what heights of consecration there are which are ours according to the Divine purpose and according to the fullness of God's gift! It is meant, and it is possible, and well within the reach of every Christian soul, that he or she should live, day by day, in the continual and utter surrender of himself or herself to the will of God, and should say, "I do the little I can do, and leave the rest with Thee"; and should say again, "All is right that seems most wrong if it be His sweet will." But instead of this absolute submission and completeness and joyfulness of surrender of ourselves to Him, what do we find? Reluctance to obey, regret at providences, Self dominant or struggling hard against the partial domination of the will of God in our hearts. The mind which was in Jesus Christ, who was able to say, "It is written of me, lo! I come to do thy will, O Lord!" is ours by virtue of our being Christians; but, alas! in practical realization how sadly it is not ours!

What noble possibilities of service, what power in the world are bestowed on Christ's people! "All power is given unto me in heaven and in earth," says He. "And he breathed on them, and said, As my Father hath sent me, even so send I you." The Divine gift to the Christian community, and to the individuals that compose it—for there are no gifts given to the community, but to the individuals that make it up—is of fullness of power for all their work. And yet look how, all through the ages, the Church has been beaten by the corruption of the world; and how today many of us are standing, either utterly careless and callous about the things that we have the medicine to cure, or in desperation looking about for other healing for the social and moral condition of the community than that which is granted to us in Jesus Christ.

"Know ye that Ramoth in Gilead is ours, and we be still, and take it not out of the hands of the King of Syria?"

There is ever so much in the world which belongs to our Master, and therefore belongs to us, and which the Church is bound to lay its hand upon and claim for its own and for its Lord's. For remember, brethren, that all the things at which I have been glancing—and I might have largely increased the catalogue—all these things—spiritual endowments of peace, and safety, and purity, and joy, of religious elevation, and consecration, and power for service, and the like—are ours by a threefold title and charter. God's purpose, which is nothing less for every one of us than that we should be "filled with all the fullness of God," and that He should supply all our need, "according to his riches in glory,"—that is the first of the parchments on which our title depends. And the second title-deed is Christ's purchase; for the efficacy of His death and the power of His triumphant life have secured for all that trust Him the whole fullness of this Divine gift. And the third of our claims and titles is the influence of that Holy Spirit that Jesus Christ gives to every one of His children to dwell in Him. There is in you, working in you, if you have any faith in that Lord, a power that is capable of making you perfectly pure, perfectly blessed, strong with an immortal strength, and glad with a "joy that is unspeakable and full of glory."

Oh, then, let us think of the awful contrast between what is ours and what we have. It is ours by the Divine intention, by the Divine gift in its fullness and all-sufficiency, and yet think of the poor, partial realization of it that has passed into our experience. Be sure that you have what you have, and that you make your own what God has made yours.

II. Then, let me suggest, again, how our text hints for us, not only the difference between possession and realization, but also our strange contentment in imperfect possession.

Ahab's remonstrances with his servants, which make the starting point of my remarks, seem to suggest that there were two reasons for their acquiescence in the domination of a foreign power on a bit of their soil. They had not realized that Ramoth was theirs, and they were too lazy and cowardly to go to take it. Ignorance of the fullness of the gift, and slothful timidity in daring everything in the effort to make it ours, explain a great deal of the present condition of Christian people.

Is not that condition of passive acquiescence in their small present attainments, and of careless indifference to the great stretch of the unattained, the characteristic of the mass of professing Christians? They have got a foothold on a new continent, and their possession of it is like the world's knowledge of the map of Africa when we were children, which had a settlement dotted here and there along the coast, and all the broad regions of the interior were blank. The settlers huddle together upon the fringe of barren sand by the salt water, and never dream of pressing forward into the heart of the land. And so, too, many of us are content with what we have got, a little bit of God, when we might have Him all; a settlement on the fringe and edge of the land, when we might traverse the whole length of it; and behold! it is all ours.

That unfamiliarity with the thought of unattained possibilities in the Christian life is a damning curse of thousands of people who call themselves Christians. They do not think, they never realize—and some of us are guilty in this respect—they never realize that it is possible for them to be all unlike what they are now, and that, instead of the miserable partial hallowing of their nature, and the poor, weak—I was going to say strength, but it is not worth calling strength, that they possess, they might be as the angels of God: "the weakest as David" and David as the very messenger of heaven itself. Why is it, why is it that there is this unfamiliarity?

And then, another reason for the woeful disproportion between what we have and what we utilize is the love of ease, such as kept these Israelites from going up to Ramoth-Gilead. It was a long way off; there was a river to be forded; there were heights to be climbed; there were weary marches to be taken; there were hard knocks going in front of the walls of Ramoth before they got inside it; and on the whole it was more comfortable to sit at home, or to look after their farms and their merchandise, than to embark on the quixotic attempt to win back a city that had not been theirs for ever so long, and that they had got on very well without.

And so it is with hosts of us Christian people; we do not realize how much we have that we never get any good out of. And, in the second place, we had rather just stay where we are, and make the best of the world as it is, and the desires of our hearts go in another direction than for our increase in the grace and knowledge of our Lord and Saviour. Ah, brethren, if we had a claim to some great property, or anything else that we really cared about, should we be so very indifferent as to asserting our rights? Should we not fight to the death, some of us, for the last inch of soil, for the last ounce of treasure that belonged to us? When you really value a thing, you secure the greatest possible amount of it; and there is very little margin between what you own and what you use.

And if there is such a tremendous difference between the breadth of the one and the narrowness of the other in our Christian life, there can be no reason for it except this, that we do not care enough about spiritual blessings and forces to make the effort that is needed to win and keep, and get the good of all that is ours.

And is not that something like despising the birthright? Is it not a criminal thing for Christian people thus to neglect, and to put aside, and never to seek to obtain, all these great gifts of God? There they lie at our doors, and they are ours for the taking. Suppose a carrier brought you a whole wagon full of precious goods, and put them down at your door, and you were not at the trouble to open your doors, or to carry the goods into your cellars. That would not look as if you cared much either for the goods or for the giver. And I wonder how many of us are chargeable with that criminal despising of God's gifts, which is clearly the explanation of our letting them lie rotting, as it were, at our gates. We are starving; paupers in the midst of plenty.

"My God shall supply all your need according to his riches in glory, by Christ Jesus," say Paul. You have the right to them all. Draw cheques against the capital that is lodged in your name in that great bank.

III. And so, lastly, my text suggests the effort that is needed to make our own ours.

"We be still, and take it not out of the hands of the King of Syria." Then these things that are ours, by God's gift, by Christ's purchase, by the Spirit's influence, will need our effort to secure them. And that is no contradiction, nor any paradox. God does exactly in the same way with regard to a great many of His natural gifts as He does with regard to His spiritual ones. He gives them to us, but we hold them on this tenure, that we put forth our best efforts to get and to keep them. His giving them does not set aside our taking. However much we tried we could not take them out of His hand if it were clenched. Open as His hand is, and stretched out to us as it is, the gifts that sparkle in it are not transferred to our hands unless we ourselves put forth an effort. So let me say that one large part of the discipline by which men make their own their own is by familiarizing themselves with the thought of the larger possibilities of unattained possessions which God has given them. That is true in everything. To recognize our present imperfection, and to see stretching before us glorious and immense possibilities, opening out into a vista where our eyesight fails us to travel to its end, is the very salt of life in every region. Artist, student, all of us "are saved by hope," in a very much wider sense than the Apostle meant by that great saying. And whosoever has once lost, or found becoming dim, the vision before him of a possible better than his present best, in any region, is in that region condemned to grow no more. If we desire to have any kind of advancement, it is only possible for us, when there gleams ever before us the untraveled road, and we see at the end of it unattained brightnesses and blessings.

And we Christian people have an endless prospect of that sort stretching before us. Oh, if we looked at it oftener, "having respect unto the recompense of the reward," we should find it easier to dash at any Ramoth-Gilead, and get it out of the hands of the strongest of the enemies that may bar our way to it. Let us familiarize ourselves with the thought of our present imperfection, and of our future, and of the possibilities which may become actualities, even here and now; and let us not fitfully use what power we have, but make the best of what graces are ours, and enjoy and expatiate in the spiritual blessings of peace and rest which Christ has already given to us. "To him that hath shall be given." And the surest way to lose what we have is to neglect the increasing of it.

And, above all, let us keep nearer to our Master, will and live more in fellowship with our Lord, and that help us to deny ourselves to ungodliness and worldly lusts. It is the prevalence of these, and the absence of self-denial, that ruins most of the Christian lives that are ruined in this world. If a man wants to be what he is not, he must cease to be what he is.

Self-sacrifice, and the emptying of our hearts of trash and trifles, is the only way to get our hearts filled with God and with His blessing. Let us keep near Jesus Christ. If we have Him for ours we have peace, we have power, we have purity. "He of God is made unto us" all in all. And every gift that may adorn humanity, and make our lives joyous and ourselves noble, is given to us in Jesus Christ. Let us put away from ourselves, then, this slothful indifference to our unattained possessions. "Know ye that Ramoth is ours?" "Let us be still" no longer. "All things are yours, whether the world, or life, or death, or things present, or things to come: all are yours if ye are Christ's."

O Lord, our gracious Father! we bless Thee that the door into Thy presence-chamber is always open to us, and Thine ear ever ready to hear the least voice. May our ears be ready to hear Thy faintest whisper.

Give us now, O Lord! some message which may have the demonstration and power of Thy Spirit. Thou knowest our weakness and our unfitness to hear or to speak, worthily to set forth and to receive Thy holy Word. But we would trust ourselves in Thy hands, and pray for that Spirit which Thou hast promised to them that wait upon Thee, that we may have given to us the word in season for all, and that we may receive and profit by the message of Thy grace. Pour out Thy holy influences upon us as a congregation of professing Christians. Grant that Thy servants may live their Christianity without ostentation and without hypocrisy, and may so walk before men that they may glorify their Father in Heaven.

Bless all Christian communions and all who, in any fashion or form, are seeking after Thee if haply they may find Thee, and trying to help their fellows in any way to live more worthy of God and of His love. Be with all Thy people this day everywhere. Let the many prayers that go up rise from faithful hearts and enter into the hearing ear of our faithful God.

Look upon us now, O Lord! We pray for all that we have failed to ask. Do Thou mercifully bestow, and answer our petitions, for the sake of Jesus Christ our Lord and Saviour. Amen.[2]

---

[2] From *Pulpit Prayers*.

HOW WE KNOW LOVE [1]

There be two kinds of knowledge: the mere rattle of notions in a man's brain, like the seeds of a withered poppy head; very many, very dry, very hard; that will make a noise when you shake it. And there is another kind of knowledge, which goes deep down into the heart, and is the only knowledge worth calling by the name; and that knowledge is the child of love.

Love, says Paul, is the parent of all knowledge. Well, now, can we find any illustrations from similar facts in other regions? Yes! I think so. How do we know, really know, any emotions of any sort whatever? Only by experience. The poets of the world have been singing about love ever since the world began. But no heart has learned what love is from even the sweetest and deepest songs. Only the lips that have drunk the cup of sweetness or of bitterness can tell how sweet or how bitter it is, and even when they, made wise by experience, speak out their deepest hearts, the listeners are but little the wiser unless they, too, have been initiated in the same school. Experience is our only teacher, and her school fees are heavy.

---

[1] From *Similes and Figures from Alexander Maclaren,* by Francis E. Clark. Copyright, 1910, by Fleming H. Revell, and reprinted by permission.

4. "AS I HAVE LOVED" [1]

"A new commandment I give unto you, that ye love one another; as I have loved you, that ye also love one another. By this shall all men know that ye are My disciples, if ye love one to another." JOHN 13:34, 35.

Wishes from dying lips are sacred. They sink deep into memories and mold faithful lives. The sense of impending separation had added an unwonted tenderness to our Lord's address, and He had designated His disciples by the fond name of "little children." The same sense here gives authority to His words, and molds them into the shape of a command. The disciples had held together because He was in their midst. Will the arch stand when the keystone is struck out? Will not the spokes fall asunder when the nave of the wheel is taken away? He would guard them from the disintegrating tendencies that were sure to set in when He was gone; and He would point them to a solace for His absence, and to a kind of substitute for His presence. For to love the brethren whom they see would be, in some sense, a continuing to love the Christ whom they had ceased to see. And so, immediately after He said: "Whither I go ye cannot come," He goes on to say: "Love one another as I have loved you."

He called this a "new commandment," though to love one's neighbor as one's self was a familiar commonplace amongst the Jews, and had a recognized position in Rabbinical teaching. But His commandment proposed a new object of love, it set forth a new measure of love, so greatly different from all that had preceded it as to become almost a new kind of love, and it suggested and supplied a new motive power for love. This commandment "could give life" and fulfill itself. Therefore it comes to us as a "new commandment"—even to us—and, unlike the

---
[1] From *Last Sheaves*, American Tract Society, 1904. Reprinted by permission.

words which preceded it, which we were considering in former sermons, it is wholly and freshly applicable today as in the ages that are passed. I ask you, first, to consider—
I. The new scope of the new commandment.

"Love one another." The newness of the precept is realized, if we think for a moment of the new phenomenon which obedience to it produced. When the words were spoken, the then-known civilized Western world was cleft by great, deep gulfs of separation, like the crevasses in a glacier, by the side of which our racial animosities and class differences are merely superficial cracks on the surface. Language, religion, national animosities, differences of condition, and saddest of all, difference of sex, split the world up into alien fragments. A "stranger" and an "enemy" were expressed in one language, by the same word. The learned and the unlearned, the slave and his master, the barbarian and the Greek, the man and the woman, stood on opposite sides of the gulfs, flinging hostility across. A Jewish peasant wandered up and down for three years in His own little country, which was the very focus of narrowness and separation and hostility, as the Roman historian felt when he called the Jews the "haters of the human race"; He gathered a few disciples, and He was crucified by a contemptuous Roman governor, who thought that the life of one fanatical Jew was a little price to pay for popularity with his troublesome subjects, and in a generation after, the clefts were being bridged, and all over the empire a strange new sense of unity was being breathed, and Barbarian, Scythian, bond and free, male and female, Jew and Greek, learned and ignorant, clasped hands and sat down at one table, and felt themselves all one in Christ Jesus. They were ready to break all other bonds, and to yield to the uniting forces that streamed out from His Cross. There never had been anything like it. No wonder that the world began to babble about sorcery, and conspiracies, and complicity in unnamable vices. It was only that the disciples were obeying the "new commandment," and a new thing had come into the world—a community held together by love and not by geographical accidents or linguistic affinities, or the iron fetters of the conqueror. You sow the seed in furrows separated by ridges, and the ground is seamed, but when the seed springs, the ridges are hidden, no division appears, and as far as the eye can reach, the cornfield stretches, rippling in unbroken waves of gold. The new commandment made a new thing, and the world wondered.

Now then, brethren, do not let us forget that, although it is in some respects a great deal harder today than it was then, to obey this commandment, the diverse circumstances in which Christian individuals and Christian communities are this day placed may modify the form of our obedience, but do not in the smallest degree weaken the obligation, for the individual Christian and for the societies of Christians, to follow this commandment. The multiplication of numbers, the cessation of the armed hostility of the world, the great varieties in intellectual position in regard to the truths of Christianity, divergencies of culture, and many other things, are separating forces. But our Christianity is worth very little, if it cannot master these separating tendencies, even as in the early days of freshness, the Christianity that sprang in these new converts' minds mastered the far more powerful separating tendencies with which they had to contend.

Every Christian man is under the obligation to recognize his kindred with every other Christian man—his kindred in the deep foundations of his spiritual being, which are far deeper, and ought to be far more operative in drawing together, than the superficial differences of culture or opinion or the like, which may part us. The bond that holds Christian men together is their common relation to the one Lord, and that ought to influence their attitude to one another. You say I am talking commonplaces. Yes; and the condition of Christianity this day is the sad and tragical sign that the commonplaces need to be talked about, till they are rubbed into the conscience of the Church as they never have been before.

Do not let us suppose that Christian love is mere sentiment. I shall have to speak a word or two about that presently, but I would fain lift the whole subject, if I can, out of the region of mere unctuous words, and gush of half-feigned emotion, which mean nothing, and would make you feel that it is a very practical commandment, gripping us hard, when our Lord says to us, "Love one another."

I have spoken about the accidental conditions which make obedience to this commandment difficult. The real reason which makes the obedience to it difficult is the slackness of our own hold on the center. In the measure in which we are filled with Jesus Christ, in that measure will that expression of His Spirit and His life become natural to us. Every Christian has affinities with every other Christian, in the depths of his being, so as that he is a great deal more like his brother, who is possessor of "like precious faith," however unlike the two may be in outlook, in idiosyncrasy, and culture and in creed, than he is to another man with whom he may have a far closer sympathy in all these matters than he has with the brother in question, but from whom he is parted by this; that the one trusts and loves and obeys Jesus Christ, and the other does not. So, for individual and for churches, the commandment takes this shape—Go down to the depths and you will find that you are closer to the Christian man or community which seems farthest from you, than you are to the non-Christian who seems nearest to you. Therefore, let your love follow your kinship, and your heart recognize the oneness that knits you together. That is a revolutionary commandment; what would become of our present organizations of Christianity if it were obeyed? That is a revolutionary commandment; what would become of our individual relations to the whole family who, in every place, and in many tongues, and with many creeds, call on Jesus as on their Lord—their Lord and ours? I leave you to answer the question. Only, I say the commandment has for its first scope all who, in every place, love the Lord Jesus Christ.

But there is more than that involved in it. The very principle which makes this love to one another imperative upon all disciples makes it equally imperative upon every follower of Jesus Christ to embrace in a real affection all whom Jesus so loved as to die for them. If I am to love a Christian man because he and I love Christ, I am to love everybody, because Christ loves me and everybody, and because He died on the Cross for me and for all men. And so one of the other Apostles, or, at least, the letter which goes by his name, laid hold on the true connection when, instead of concentrating Christian affection on the Church, and letting the world go to the devil as an alien thing, he said: "Add to your faith," this, that, and the other, and "brotherly kindness, and to brotherly kindness, charity." The particular does not exclude the general, it leads to the general. The fire kindled upon the hearth gives warmth to all the chamber. The circles are concentric, and the widest sweep is struck from the same middle point as the narrow. So the new commandment does not cut humanity in two halves, but gathers all diversity into one, and spreads the great reconciling of Christian love over all the antagonisms and oppositions of earth. Let me ask you to notice.

II. The example of the new commandment, "As I have loved you."

That solemn "as" lifts itself up before us, shines far ahead of us, ought to draw us to itself in hope, and not to repel us from itself in despair. "As I have loved"—what a tremendous thing for a man to stand up before his fellows, and say, "Take Me as the perfect Example of perfect love; and let My example—undimmed by the mists of gathering centuries, and unweakened by the change of condition, and circumstance, fresh as ever after ages have passed, and closely-fitting as ever in all varieties of human character and condition—stand before you; the ideal that I have realized, and that you will be blessed in the proportion that you seek, though you fail to realize it!" There is, I venture to believe, only one aspect of Jesus Christ in which such a setting forth of Himself as the perfect Incarnation of perfect love is warrantable; and that is found in the old belief that His very birth was the result of His love, and that His death was the climax of that love. And if so, we have to turn to Bethlehem, and the whole life, and the Cross at its end, as being the Christ-given example and model for our love to our brethren.

What do we see there? I have said that there is too much of mere sickly sentimentality about the ordinary treatment of this great commandment, and that I desired to lift it out of that region into a far nobler, more strenuous, and difficult one. This is what we see in that life and in that death: First of all, the activity of love—"Let *us* not love in words, but in deed and in truth." Then we see the self-forgetfulness of love—"Even Christ pleased not himself." Then we see the self-sacrifice of love—"Greater love hath no man than this, that a man lay down his life for his friends." And in these three points, on which I would fain enlarge if I might, active love, self-oblivious love, self-sacrificing love, you have the pattern set for us all. Christian love is no mere sickly maiden, full of sentimental emotions and honeyed words. She is a strenuous virgin, girt for service, a heroine ready for dangers, and prepared to be a martyr if it be needful. Love's language is sacrifice. "I give Thee myself," is its motto. And that is the pattern that is set before us all—"as I have loved you."

I have tried to show you how the commandment was new in many particulars, and it is for ever new in this particular, that it is for ever before us, unattained, and drawing faithful hearts to itself, and ever opening out into new heroisms, and, therefore, blessedness, of self-sacrifice, and ever leading us to confess the differences, deep, tragic, sinful, between us and Him Who—we sometimes think too presumptuously—we venture to say is our Lord and Master.

Did you ever see in some great picture gallery a copyist sitting in front of a Raffaello, and comparing his poor feeble daub, all out of drawing, and with little of the Divine beauty that the master had breathed over his canvas, even if it preserved the mere mechanical outline? That is what you and I should do with our lives: take them and put them down side by side with the original. We shall have to do it some day. Had we better not do it now, and try to bring the copy a little nearer to the masterpiece; and let that "as I have loved you" shine before us and draw us on to unattainable heights?

And now, lastly, we have here

III. The motive-power for obedience to the commandment.

And that is as new as all the rest. That "as" expresses the manner of the love, but it also expresses the motive and the power. It might be translated into the equivalent "in the fashion in which," or it might be translated into the equivalent "since—" "I have loved you." The original might bear the rendering, "that ye also *may* love one another." That is to say, what keeps men from obeying this commandment is the instinctive self-regard which is natural to us all. There are muscles in the body which are so constructed that they close tightly; and the heart is something like one of these sphincter muscles—it shuts by nature, especially if there has been anything put inside it over which it can shut and keep it all to itself. But there is one thing that dethrones Self, and enthrones the angel Love in a heart, and that is—that into that heart there shall come surging the sense of the great love wherewith "I have loved you." That melts the iceberg, nothing else will.

That love of Christ to us, received into our hearts, and there producing an answering love to Him, will make us, in the measure in which we live in it and let it rule us, love everything and every person that He loves. That love of Jesus Christ, stealing into our hearts and there sweetening the ever-springing "issues of life," will make them flow out in glad obedience to any commandment of His. That love of Jesus Christ, received into our hearts, and responded to by our answering love, will work, as love always does, a magical transformation. A great monastic teacher wrote his precious book about *The Imitation of Christ*. "Imitation" is a great word, "Transformation" is a greater. "We all," receiving on the mirror of our loving hearts the love of Jesus Christ, "are changed into the same likeness." Thus, then, the love, which is our pattern, is also our motive and our power for obedience, and the more we bring ourselves under its influences, the more we shall love all those who are beloved by, and lovers of, Jesus.

That is the one foundation for a world knit together in the bonds of amity and concord. There have been attempts at brotherhood, and the guillotine has ended what was begun in the name of "fraternity." Men build towers, but there is no cement between the bricks, unless the love of Christ holds them together; and therefore Babel after Babel comes down about the ears of its builders. But notwithstanding all that is dark today, and though the war clouds are lowering, and the hearts of men are inflamed with fierce passions, Christ's commandment is Christ's promise; and though the vision tarry, it will surely come. So even today Christian men ought to stand for Christ's peace, and for Christ's love. The old commandment which we have had from the beginning, is the new commandment that fits today as it fits all the ages. It is a dream, say some. Yet, a dream; but a morning dream which comes true. Let us do the little we can to make it true, and to bring about the day when the flock of men will gather round the one Shepherd, Who loved them to the death, and Who has bid them and helped them, to "love one another as"—and since—"He has loved them."

O Lord, our God and Father! we would come to Thee with thankful petitions and with thankfulness that expects in the future as well as praises for the past.

We draw near to Thee now with humble praise for all Thy great mercy and goodness to us, manifested to us in more ways than our treacherous memories can recall, and continued to us notwithstanding all our ill desserts, and our many wanderings and our much misuse of Thy many benefits.

We thank Thee for undeserved mercies. We thank Thee for the continuance of often misused benefits. We thank Thee that Thou dost not pluck away our joys when we forget the Hand that gives them, but that Thou dost continue with patience, endless because it is Divine, wooing us to Thyself, and hoping that the mercy of God may lead us to repentance.

Let Thy grace be upon each of us here before Thee in all our different conditions and avocations; and do Thou guide us all by Thy counsel, and help us to stay our hearts upon Thyself, and to love Thee fully, and constantly to realize the presence of the peace that comes from Jesus Christ our Saviour that nothing may draw us away from Him, and no evil may befall us. Amen.[2]

---

[2] From *Pulpit Prayers*.

THE RECORDS OF HEAVEN [1]

~~~~~~~~~~~~~~~~~~~~~~~~~~~~

The deeds that stand highest on the records in heaven are not those which we vulgarly call great. Many "a cup of cold water only" will be found to have rated higher there than jeweled golden chalices brimming with rare wines. God's treasuries, where He keeps His children's gifts, will be like many a mother's secret store of relics of her children, full of things of no value, what the world calls "trash," but precious in his eyes for the love's sake that was in them.

All service which is done from the same motive in the same force is of the same worth in His eyes. It does not matter whether you have the gospel in a penny Testament printed on thin paper with black ink, and done up in cloth, or in an illuminated missal glowing in gold and color, painted with loving care on fair parchment, and bound in jeweled ivory. And so it matters little about the material or the scale on which we express our devotion and our aspirations; all depends on what we copy, not on the size of the canvas on which, or on the material in which, we copy it. "Small service is true service while it lasts," and the unnoticed insignificant servants may do work every whit as good and noble as the most widely known, to whom have been intrusted by Christ tasks that mold the ages.

---

[1] From *Similes and Figures from Alexander Maclaren*, by Francis E. Clark. Copyright, 1910, by Fleming H. Revell, and reprinted by permission.

5. THE SECRET OF IMMORTAL YOUTH [1]

"Even the youths shall faint and be weary, and the young men shall utterly fall. But they that wait upon the Lord shall renew their strength; they shall mount up with wings as eagles; they shall run and not be weary; and they shall walk and not faint." Isa. 40:30, 31.

I remember a sunset at sea, where the bosom of each wavelet that fronted the west was aglow with fiery gold, and the back of each turned eastward was cold green; so that, looking on the one hand all was glory, and on the other all was sober melancholy. So differently does life look to you young people and to us older ones. Every man must buy his own experience for himself, and no preaching nor talking will ever make you see life as we see it. It is neither possible nor desirable that you should; but it is both possible and most desirable that you should open your eyes to plain, grave facts, which do not at all depend on our way of looking at things, and that if they be ascertainable, as they are, you should let them shape your life.

Here are a couple of facts in my text which I want you to look steadily in the face, and to take account of them, because, if you do so now, they may save you an immense deal of disappointment and sorrow in the days that are to come. You have the priceless prerogative still in your hands of determining what that future is to be; but you will never use that power rightly if you are guided by illusions, or if, unguided by anything but inclination, you let things drift, and do as you like.

So then, my object is simply to deal with these two forecasts which my text presents; the one a dreary certainty of weariness and decay, the other a blessed possibility of inexhaustible and incorruptible strength

---
[1] From *The Unchanging Christ*, Alexander & Shepheard (London), 1889.

and youth, and on the contrast to build as earnest an appeal to you as I can make.

I. Now, then, first look at the first fact here, that of the dreary certainty of weariness and decay.

I do not need to spend much time in talking about that. It is one of the commonplaces which are so familiar that they have lost all power of impression, and can only be rescued from their trivial insignificance by being brought into immediate connection with our own experience. If, instead of the toothless generality, "the youths shall faint and be weary," I could get you young people to say, *"I—I* shall faint and be weary, and, as sure as I am living, I shall lose what makes to me the very joy of life at this moment," I should not have preached in vain.

Of course the words of my text point to the plain fact that all created and physical life, by the very law of its being, in the act of living tends to death; and by the very operation of its strength tends to exhaustion. There are three stages in every creature's life—that of growth, that of equilibrium, that of decay. You are in the first. If you live you will come to the second and the third, as certain as fate. Your "eyes will grow dim," your "natural force" will be "abated," the body will become a burden, the years that are full of buoyancy will be changed for years of heaviness and weariness, strength will decay, "and the young men" —that is you—"shall utterly fall."

And the text points also to another fact, that, long before your natural life shall have begun to tend toward decay, hard work and occasional sorrows and responsibilities and burdens of all sorts will very often make you wearied and ready to faint. In your early days you dream of life as a kind of enchanted garden, full of all manner of delights; and you stand at the threshold with eager eyes and outstretched hands. Ah! dear young friend, long before you have traversed the length of one of its walks, you will often have been sick and tired of the whole thing, and weary of what is laid upon you.

My text points to another fact, as certain as gravitation, that the faintness and weariness and decay of the bodily strength will be accompanied with a parallel change in your feelings. We are drawn onward by hopes, and when we get them fulfilled we find that they are disappointing. Custom, which weighs upon us "heavy as frost, and deep almost as life," takes the edge off everything that is delightsome, though it does not so completely take away the pain of things that are burdensome and painful. Men travel from a tinted morning into the sober light of common day, and with failing faculties and shattered illusions and dissipated hopes, and powers bending under the long monotony of middle life, most of them live. Now all that is the veriest threadbare morality, and I daresay while I have been talking some of you have been thinking that I am repeating platitudes that every old woman could preach. So I am. That is to say, I am trying to put into feeble words the universal human experience. That is *your* experience, and what I want to get you to think about now is that, as sure as you are living and rejoicing in your youth and strength, this is the fate that is awaiting you—"the youths shall faint and be weary, and shall utterly fall."

Well, then, one question, Do you not think that, if that is so, it would be as well to face it? Do you not think that a wise man would take account of all the elements in forecasting his life, and would shape his conduct accordingly? If there be something certain to come, it is a very questionable piece of wisdom to make that the thing which we are most unwilling to think about. I do not want to take anything out of the happy buoyancy of youth. I would say, as even that cynical, bitter Ecclesiastes says, "Rejoice, O young man, in thy youth; and let thy heart cheer thee in the days of thy youth." By all means, only take all the facts into account, and if you have joys which shrivel up at the touch of this thought, then the sooner you get rid of such joys the better. If your gladness depends upon your forcibly shutting your eyes to what is inevitably certain to come about, do you not think that you are living in a fool's paradise that you had better get out of as soon as possible? There is the fact. Will you be a wise and brave man and front it, and settle how you are going to deal with it, or will you let it hang there on your horizon, a thunder cloud that you do not like to look at, and that you are all the more unwilling to entertain the thought of, because you are so sure that it will burst in storm? Lay this, then, to heart, though it be a dreary certainty, that weariness and decay are sure to be your fate.

II. Now turn, in the next place, to the blessed opposite possibility of inexhaustible and immortal strength. "They that wait upon the Lord shall renew their strength; they shall mount up with wings as eagles; they shall run and not be weary; they shall walk and not faint."

The life of nature tends inevitably downward, but there may be another life within the life of nature, which shall have the opposite motion, and tend as certainly upward. "The youths shall faint and be weary." Whether they be Christians or not, the law of decay and fatigue will act upon them; but there may be that within each of us, if we will, which shall resist that law, and have no proclivity whatsoever to extinction in its blaze, to death in its life, to weariness in its effort, and shall be replenished and not exhausted by expenditure. "They that wait upon the Lord shall renew their strength," and, in all forms of motion possible to a creature, they shall expatiate and never tire. So let us look on this blessed possibility a little more closely.

Note, then, how to get at it. "They that wait upon the Lord" is Old Testament dialect for what in New Testament phraseology is meant by "Believe on the Lord Jesus Christ." For the notion expressed here by "waiting" is that of expectant dependence, and the New Testament "faith" is the very same in its attitude of expectant dependence, while the object of the Old Testament "waiting," Jehovah, is identical with the object of the New Testament faith, which fastens on God manifest in the flesh, the Man Jesus Christ.

Therefore, I am not diverting the language of my text from its true meaning, but simply opening its depth, when I say that the condition of the inflow of this unwearied and immortal life into our poor, fainting, dying humanity is simply the trust in Jesus Christ the Redeemer of our souls. True, the revelation has advanced, the contents of that which we grasp are more developed and articulate, blessed be God! True, we know more about Jehovah, when we see Him in Jesus Christ, than Isaiah did. True, we have to trust in Him as dying on the Cross for our salvation and as the pattern and example in His humanity of all nobleness and beauty of life for young or old, but the Christ is the "same yesterday, and today, and for ever." And the faith that knit the furthest back of the saints of old to the Jehovah, whom they dimly knew, is in essence identical with the faith that binds my poor, sinful heart to the Christ that died and that lives for my redemption and salvation. So, dear brethren, here is the simple old message for each of you, young or old. No matter where we stand on the course of life, there may come into our hearts a Divine Indweller, who laughs at weariness and knows nothing of decay; and He will come if, as sinful men, we turn ourselves to that dear Lord, who fainted and was weary many a time in His humanity, and who now lives, the "strong Son of God, immortal love," to make us partakers in His immortality and His strength. How, then, we get this Divine gift is by faith in Jesus Christ, which is the expansion, as it was the root, of trust in Jehovah.

Further, what is this strength that we thus get, if we will, by faith? It is the true entrance into our souls of a Divine life. God in His Son will come to us, according to His own gracious and profound promise: "If any man open the door I will enter in." He will come into our hearts and abide there. He will give to us a life derived from, and, therefore, kindred with, His own. And in that connection it is very striking to notice how the prophet, in the context, reiterates these two words, "*fainteth* not, neither is *weary*." He begins by speaking of "God, the Lord, the Creator of the ends of the earth, who fainteth not, neither is weary." He passes on to speak of His gift of power to the faint. He returns to the contrast between the Creator's incorruptible strength and the fleeting power of the strongest and youngest. And then he crowns all with the thought that the same characteristics shall mark them in whom the unwearied God dwells, as mark Him. We, too, like Him, if we have Christ in our hearts by faith, shall share, in some fashion and degree, in His wondrous prerogative of unwearied strength.

So, brethren, here is the promise. God will give Himself to you, and in the very heart of your decaying nature will plant the seed of an immortal being which shall, like His own, shake off fatigue from the limbs, and never tend to dissolution or an end. The life of nature dies by living; the life of grace, which may belong to us all, lives by living, and lives evermore thereby. And so that life is continuous and progressive, with no tendency to decay, nor term to its being. "The path of the just is as the shining light that shineth more and more" until it riseth to the zenith of the noontide of the day. Each of you, looking forward to the certain ebbing away of creatural power, to the certain changes that may pass upon you, may say, "I know that I shall have to leave behind me my present youthful strength, my unworn freshness, my buoyancy, my confidence, my wonder, my hope; but I shall carry my Christ; and in Him I shall possess the secret of an immortal youth."

The oldest angels are the youngest. The longer men live in fellowship with Christ the stronger do they grow. And though our lives, whether we be Christians or no, are necessarily subject to the common laws of mortality; we may carry all that is worth preserving of the earliest stages into the latest; and when gray hairs are upon us, and we are living next door to our graves, we may still have the enthusiasm, the energy, and above all, the boundless hopefulness that made the gladness and the spring of our long-buried youth. "They shall still bring forth fruit in old age." "The youths shall faint and be weary, but they that wait upon the Lord shall renew their strength."

There is one more point to touch, and then I have done, and that is the manner in which this immortal strength is exercised. The latter clauses of my text give us, so to speak, three forms of motion. "They shall mount up with wings as eagles." Some good commentators find in this a parallel to the words in the 103rd Psalm, "My youth is renewed like the eagle's," and propose to translate it in this fashion, "They shall cast their plumage like the eagle." But it seems much more in accordance with the context and the language to adopt substantially the reading of our English version here, or to make the slight change, "They shall lift up their wings as the eagle," implying, of course, the steady, upward flight toward the light of heaven.

So, then, there are three forms of unwearied strength lying ready for you, young men and women, to take for your very own if you like, strength to soar, strength to run, strength to walk.

There is strength to soar. Old men generally shed their wings, and can only manage to crawl. They have done with romance. Enthusiasms are dead. Sometimes they cynically smile at their own past selves and their dreams. And it is a bad sign when an old man does that. But for the most part they are content, unless they have got Christ in their hearts, to keep along the low levels, and their soaring days are done. But if you and I have Jesus Christ for the life of our spirits, as certainly as fire sends its shooting tongues upwards, so certainly shall we rise above the sorrows and sins and cares of this "dim spot which men call earth," and find an ampler field for buoyant motion high up in communion with God. Strength to soar means the gracious power of bringing all heaven into our grasp, and setting our affections on things above. As the night falls, and joys become fewer and life sterner, and hopes become rarer and more doubtful, it is something to feel that, however straitened may be the ground below, there is plenty of room above, and that, though we are strangers upon earth, we can lift our thoughts yonder. If there be darkness here, still we can "outsoar the shadow of our night," and live close to the sun in fellowship with God. Dear brethren, life on earth were too wretched unless it were possible to "mount up with wings as eagles."

Again, you may have strength to run—that is to say, there is power waiting for you for all the great crises of your lives which call for special, though it may be brief, exertion. Such crises will come to each of you, in sorrow, work, difficulty, hard conflicts. Moments will be sprung upon you without warning, in which you will feel that years hang on the issue of an instant. Great tasks will be clashed down before you unexpectedly which will demand the gathering together of all your power. And there is only one way to be ready for such times as these, and that is to live waiting on the Lord, near Christ, with Him in your hearts, and then nothing will come that will be too big for you. However rough the road, and however severe the struggle, and however swift the pace, you will be able to keep it up. Though it may be with panting lungs and a throbbing heart, and dim eyes and quivering muscles, yet if you wait on the Lord you will run and not be weary. You will be masters of the crises.

Strength to walk may be yours—that is to say, patient power for persistent pursuit of weary, monotonous duty. That is the hardest, and so it comes last. Many a man finds it easy, under the pressure of strong excitement, and for a moment or two, to keep up a swift pace, who finds it very hard to keep steadily at unexciting work. And yet there is nothing to be done except by doggedly plodding along the dusty road of trivial duties, unhelped by excitement and unwearied by monotony. Only one thing will conquer the disgust at the wearisome round of mill-horse tasks which, sooner or later, seizes all godless men, and that is to bring the great principles of the Gospel into them, and to do them in the might and for the sake of the dear Lord. "They shall run and not be weary, they shall walk"—along life's common way in cheerful godliness, "and they shall not faint."

Dear friends, life to us all is, and must be, full of sorrow and of effort. Constant work and frequent sorrows wear us all out, and bring us many a time to the verge of fainting. I beseech you to begin right, and not to add to the other occasions for weariness that of having to retrace, with remorseful heart and ashamed feet, the paths of evil on which you have run. Begin right—that is to say, begin with Christ and take Him for Inspiration, for Pattern, for Guide, for Companion. "Run with patience the race set before you, looking unto Jesus the Author of your faith, lest ye be wearied and faint in your minds."

And if you have Him in your hearts, then, however the creatural power may be weary, yet because He is with you "your shoes shall be iron and brass, and as your day so shall your strength be"; and you may lift up in your turn the glad triumphant acknowledgment: "For this cause we, feeble as we are, faint not, but though our outward man perish, our inward man is renewed day by day."

God bless you all, and make that your experience!

O Lord, our gracious Father! Thou hast set us the example of overcoming evil with good.

We pray Thee to help us in all our daily duties and discipline, and to guide us by Thy gracious counsel step by step along our earthly paths. We thank Thee that Thou dost not send us a warfare at our own charges, and hast never yet reaped where Thou didst not sow, nor demanded before Thou hadst given. We pray Thee that Thou wouldst help us thus with grace sufficient for all circumstances and duties, and wheresoever Thou dost send us, there, O Lord! make Thyself present with us, and whatsoever Thou dost lay upon us, for that, O Lord! give us strength and patience.

Guide us ever, by Thy wise counsel, and help us to keep our ears and our hearts open for the lightest whisper, and slightest indication of Thy holy will. May we not look upon the world and its providences as so many are tempted to do, forgetting the Person Who guides it all, but may we be able to see Thee in everything that befalls us, and to recognize Thee in all our changing circumstances, and to acquit ourselves in them as good soldiers of Jesus Christ, and beloved children of their Father in Heaven.

We pray Thee to hear us now, grant us Thy blessing in this hour of worship, and to manifest Thyself to each of us as we may severally require; through Jesus Christ our Lord and Saviour. Amen.[2]

[2] From *Pulpit Prayers*.

TIME THE MOTHER OF ETERNITY [1]

If here, from this dim spot which men call earth, and amid the confusion and dust and distances of this present life, we look to Him, and with unveiled faces behold Him, and here in degree and part are being changed from glory to glory, there He will turn His face upon us, and, beholding it, in righteousness, "we shall be satisfied when we awake with his likeness."

Brethren, it is for us to choose whether we shall share in Christ's dominion or be crushed by His iron scepter. It is for us to choose whether, molding our lives after His will and pattern, we shall hereafter be made like Him in completeness. It is for us to choose whether, seeing Him here, we shall, when the brightness of His coming draws near, be flooded with gladness, or whether we shall call upon the rocks and the hills to cover us from the face of Him that sitteth on the throne.

Time is the mother of Eternity. Today molds tomorrow; and, when all the todays and tomorrows have become yesterdays, they will have determined our destiny, because they will have settled our characters. Let us keep Christ's commandments, and we shall be invested with dignity and illuminated with glory and intrusted with work far beyond anything that we can conceive here, though in their furthest reach and most dazzling brightness these are but the continuation and the perfecting of the feeble beginnings of earthly conflict and service.

---

[1] From *Similes and Figures from Alexander Maclaren,* by Francis E. Clark. Copyright, 1910, by Fleming H. Revell, and reprinted by permission.

6. RIVER AND ROCK [1]

"The world passeth away, and the lust thereof; but he that doeth the will of God abideth for ever." I JOHN 2:17.

John has been solemnly giving a charge not to love the world, nor the things that are in it. That charge was addressed to "children," "young men," "fathers." Whether these designations be taken as referring to the growth and maturity of Christian experience, or of natural life, they equally carry the lesson that no age and no stage is beyond the danger of being drawn away by the world's love, or beyond the need of the solemn dehortation therefrom.

My text is the second of the reasons which the Apostle gives for his earnest charge. We all, therefore, need it, and we always need it; though, this evening, on the last Sunday of another year, it may be more than usually appropriate to turn our thoughts in its direction. "The world passeth away, and the lust thereof." Let us lay that handful of snow on our fevered foreheads and cool our desires.

Now, there are but two things set forth in this text which is a great and wonderful antithesis between something which is in perpetual flux and passage and something which is permanent. If I might venture to cast the two thoughts into metaphorical form, I should say that here are a river and a rock. The one, the sad truth of sense, universally believed and as universally forgotten; the other, the glad truth of faith; so little regarded or operative in men's lives.

I ask you, then, to look with me for a few moments at each of these thoughts.

I. First, then, the river, or the sad truth of sense.

Now you observe that there are two things in my text of which this transiency is predicated, the one "the world," the other "the lust thereof";

---
[1] From *The God of the Amen,* Alexander & Shepheard (London), 1891.

the one outside us, the other within us. As to the former, I need only, I suppose, remind you in a sentence that what John means by "the world" is not the material globe on which we dwell, but the whole aggregate of things visible and material, together with the lives of the men whose lives are directed to, and bounded by, that visible and material, and all considered as wrenched apart from God. That, and not the mere external physical creation, is what he means by "the world," and therefore the passing away of which he speaks is not only (although, of course, it includes) the decay and dissolution of material things, but the transiency of things which are or have to do with the visible, and are separated by us from God. Over all these, he says, there is written the sentence, "Dust thou art, and unto dust thou shalt return." There is a continual flowing on of the stream. As the original implies even more strongly than in our translation, "the world" is in the act of "passing away." Like the slow traveling of the scenes of some movable panorama which glide along, even as the eye looks upon them, and are concealed behind the side flats, before the gazer has taken in the whole picture, so equably, constantly, silently, and therefore unnoticed by us, all is in a state of continual motion. There is no *present* time. Even whilst we name the moment it dies. The drop hangs for an instant on the verge, gleaming in the sunlight, and then falls into the gloomy abyss that silently sucks up years and centuries. There is no present, but all is movement.

Brethren, that has been the commonplace of moralists and poets and preachers from the beginning of time; and it would be folly for me to suppose that I can add anything to the impressiveness of the thought. All that I want to do is to wake you up to preach it to yourselves, for that is the only thing that is of any use.

> So passeth, in the passing of an hour
> Of mortal life, the leaf, the bud, the flower.

But beside this transiency external to us, John finds a corresponding transiency within us. "The world passeth, and the lust thereof." Of course the word "lust" is employed by him in a much wider sense than in our use of it. With us it means one specific and very ugly form of earthly desire. With him it includes the whole genus—all desires of every sort more or less noble or ignoble, which have this for their characteristic that they are directed to, stimulated by, and fed or starved on, the fleeting things of this outward life. If thus a man has anchored himself to that which has no perpetual stay, so long as the cable holds he follows the fate of the thing to which he has pinned himself. And if it perish he perishes, in a very profound sense, with it. If you trust yourselves in the leaky vessel, when the water rises in *it* it will drown *you*, and you will go to the bottom with the craft to which you have trusted yourselves. If you embark in the little ship that carries Christ and His fortunes, you will come with Him to the haven.

But these fleeting desires, of which my text speaks, point to that sad feature of human experience, that we all outgrow and leave behind us, and think of very little value, the things that once to us were all but heaven. There was a time when toys and sweetmeats were our treasures, and since that day how many burnt-out hopes we all have had! How little we should know ourselves if we could go back to the fears and wishes and desires that used to agitate us ten, twenty, thirty years ago! They lie behind us, no longer part of ourselves; they have slipped away from us, and

> We all are changed, by still degrees,
> All but the basis of the soul.

The self-conscious same man abides, and yet how different the same man is! Our lives, then, will zigzag instead of keeping a straight course, if we let desires that are limited by anything that we can see guide and regulate us.

But, brethren, though it be a digression from my text, I cannot help touching for a moment upon a yet sadder thought than that. There are desires that *remain*, when the gratification of them has become impossible. Sometimes the lust outlasts the world, sometimes the world outlasts the lust; and one knows not which is the sadder. There is a hell upon earth for many of us who, having set our affections upon some creatural object, and having had that withdrawn from us, are ready to say, "They have taken away my gods! And what shall I do?" And there is a hell of the same sort waiting beyond those dark gates through which we have all to pass, where men who never desired anything, except what the world that has slipped out of their reluctant fingers could give them, are shut up with impossible longings after a for ever vanished good. "Father Abraham! a drop of water; for I am tormented in this flame." That is what men come to, if the fire of their lust burn after its objects are withdrawn.

But let me remind you that this transiency of which I have been speaking receives very strange treatment from most of us. I do not know that it is altogether to be regretted that it so seldom comes to men's consciousness. Perhaps it is right that it should not be uppermost in our thoughts always; but yet there is no vindication for the entire oblivion to which we condemn it. The march of these fleeting things is like that of cavalry with their horses' feet wrapped in straw, in the night, across the snow, silent and unnoticed. We cannot realize the revolution of the earth, because everything partakes in it. We talk about standing still, and we are whirling through space with inconceivable rapidity. By a like illusion we deceive ourselves with the notion of stability, when everything about us is hastening away. Some of you do not like to be reminded of it, and think it a killjoy. You try to get rid of the thought, and hide your head in the sand, and fancy that the rest of your body presents no mark to the archer's arrow. Now, surely common sense says to all, that if there be some fact certain and plain and applying to you, which, if accepted, would profoundly modify your life, you ought to take it into account. And what I want you to do, dear friends, tonight, is to look in the face this fact, which you all acknowledge so utterly that some of you are ready to say, "What was the use of coming to a chapel to hear that threadbare old thing dinned into my ears again?" and to take it into account in shaping your lives. Have you done so? Have you? Suppose a man that lived in a land habitually shaken by earthquakes were to say, "I mean to ignore the fact; and I am going to build a house just as if there was not such a thing as an earthquake expected"; he would have it toppling about his ears very soon. Suppose a man upon the ice slopes of the Alps were to say, "I am going to ignore slipperiness and gravitation," he would before long find himself, if there was any consciousness left in him, at the bottom of a precipice, bruised and bleeding. And suppose a man says, "I am not going to take the fleetingness of the things of earth into account at all, but intend to live as if all things were to remain as they are"; what would become of him do you think? Is he a wise man or a fool? And is he *you*? He *is* some of you! "So teach us to number our days that we may apply our hearts unto wisdom."

Then, let me say to you, see that you take noble lessons out of these undeniable and all-important facts. There is one kind of lesson that I do not want you to take out of it. "Let us eat and drink, for tomorrow we die," or, to put it into a more vulgar formula, "A short life and a merry one." The mere contemplation of the transiency of earthly things may, and often does, lend itself to very ignoble conclusions, and men draw from it the thought that, as life is short, they had better crowd into it as much of sensual enjoyment as they can.

"Gather ye roses while ye may" is a very common keynote, struck by poets of the baser sort. And it is a thought that influences some of us, I have little doubt. Or there may be another consideration. "Make hay whilst the sun shines." "Hurry on your getting rich, because you have not very long to do it in"; or the like.

Now all that is supremely unworthy. The true lesson to be drawn is the plain, old one which it is never superfluous to shout into men's ears, until they have obeyed it—viz., "Set not thine heart on that which is not; and which flieth away as an eagle towards heaven." Do you, dear brother, see to it, that your roots go down through the gravel on the surface. Do you see to it that you dig deeper than that; and thrusting your hand, as it were, through the thin, silk-paper screen that stands between you and the Eternal, grasp the hand that you will find on the other side, waiting and ready to clasp you, and to hold you up.

When they build a new house in Rome they have to dig down through sometimes sixty or a hundred feet of rubbish that runs like water, the ruins of old temples and palaces, once occupied by men in the same flush of life in which we are now. We, too, have to dig down through ruins, until we get to Rock and build there, and build secure. Withdraw your affections and your thoughts and your desires from the fleeting, and fix them on the permanent. If a captain takes anything but the pole star for his fixed point he will lose his reckoning, and his ship will be on the reefs. If we take anything but God for our supreme delight and desire we shall perish.

Then let me say, too, let this thought stimulate us to crowd every moment, as full as it can be packed, with noble work and heavenly thoughts. These fleeting things are elastic, and you may put all but infinite treasure into them. Think of what the possibilities, for each of us, of this dying year were on the 1st of January; and of what the realization has been by the 28th of December. So much that we could have done; so little that we have done! So many ripples of the river have passed, bearing no golden sand to pile upon the shore! "We have been" is a sad word; but oh! the one sad word is, "We might have been." And, so, do you see to it that you fill time with that which is kindred to eternity, and make "one day as a thousand years" in the elastic possibilities and realities of consecration and of service.

Further, let the thought help us to the conviction of the relative insignificance of all that can change. That will not spoil nor shade any real joy; rather it will add to it poignancy that prevents it from cloying or from becoming the enemy of our souls. But the thought will wondrously lighten the burden that we have to carry, and the tasks which we have to perform. "But for a moment," makes all light. There was an old rabbi, long ago, whose real name was all but lost, because everybody nicknamed him "Rabbi This-also." The reason was because he had perpetually on his lips the saying about everything as it came, "This also will pass." He was a wise man. Let us go to his school and learn his wisdom.

II. Now let me say a word, and it can only be a word, about the second of the thoughts here, which I designated as the Rock, or the glad truth of Faith.

We might have expected that John's antithesis to the world that passeth would have been the God that abides. But he does not so word his sentence, although the thought of the Divine permanence underlies it. Rather over against the fleeting world he puts the abiding man who does the will of God.

Of course there is a very solemn sense in which all men, even they who have most exclusively lived for what they call the present, do last for ever, and in which their deeds do so too. After death is the judgment, and the issues of eternity depend upon the actions of time; and every fleeting thought comes back to the hand that projected it, like the Australian savage's boomerang that, flung out, returns and falls at the feet of the thrower. But that is not what John means by "abiding for ever." He means something very much more blessed and lofty than that; and the following is the course of his thought. There is only one permanent Reality in the universe, and that is God. All else is shadow and He is the substance. All else was, is, and is not. He is the One Who was, is, and is to come, the timeless and only permanent Being. The will of God is the permanent element in all changeful material things. And consequently he who does the will of God links himself with the Divine Eternity, and becomes partaker of that solemn and blessed Being which lives above mutation.

Obedience to God's will is the permanent element in human life. Whosoever humbly and trustfully seeks to mold his will after the Divine will, and to bring God's will into practice in his doings, that man has pierced through the shadows and grasped the substance, and partakes of the Immortality which he adores and serves. Himself shall live for ever in the true life which is blessedness. His deeds shall live for ever when all that lifted itself in opposition to the Divine will shall be crushed and annihilated. They shall live in His own peaceful consciousness; they shall live in the blessed rewards which they shall bring to the doers. His habits will need no change.

What will you do when you are dead? You have to go into a world where there are no gossip and no housekeeping; no mills and no offices; no shops and no books; no colleges and no sciences to learn. What will you do there? "He that doeth the will of God abideth for ever." If you have done your housekeeping, and your weaving and spinning, and your bookkeeping, and your buying and selling, and your studying, and your experimenting with a conscious reference to God, it is all right.

That has made the act capable of eternity, and there will be no need for such a man to change. The material on which he works will change, but the inner substance of his life will be unaffected by the trivial change from earth to heaven. Whilst the endless ages roll he will be doing just what he was doing down here; only here he was playing with counters, and yonder he will be trusted with gold, and dominion over ten cities. To all other men the change that comes when earth passes from them, or they from it, is as when a trench is dug across a railway, into which the express goes with a smash, and there is an end. To the man who, in the trifles of time, has been obeying the will of God, and therefore subserving eternity and his interests there, the trench is bridged, and he will go on after he crosses it just as he did before, with the same purpose, the same desires, the same submission, and the same drinking into himself of the fullness of immortal life.

Brother, John tells us that obedience to the will of God brings permanence into our fleeting years. But how are we to obey the will of God? John tells us that the only way is by love. But how are we to love God? John tells us that the only way to love—which love is the only way to obedience—is by knowing and believing the love that God hath to us. But how are we to know that God hath love to us? John tells us that the only way to know the love of God, which is the only way of our loving Him, which in its turn is the only way to obedience, which again is the only way to permanence of life, is to believe in Jesus Christ and His propitiation for our sins. The river flows on for ever, but it sweeps round the base of the Rock of Ages. And in Him, by faith in His blood, we may find our sure refuge and eternal home.

We thank Thee, O God! that still Thou dost speak with us as a man speaketh with his friend. We beseech Thee that Thou wouldst help us to respond to Thy loving heart; that we may truly be called the friends of God. We thank Thee for Thy changeless love, for Thy mighty and all-sufficient presence. We thank Thee that we may have Thee for our Companion, Counselor, Guide; for our hearts' delight and treasure in all our circumstances. We pray Thee to strengthen us that we may truly set our minds and affections on Thyself, and so use all the blessings and discharge all the duties and bear all the sorrows of this earthly life as that they may bring us and keep us nearer to Thyself.

We see Thee sometimes from afar and dimly long for Thy nearer presence. We follow our Master with faltering steps and slowly; with many a wandering from the path, and many a starting aside of heart and mind. But we beseech Thee that Thou wouldst help us in the days to come, be they more or fewer, to make straight paths for our feet, and to follow the Lamb whithersoever He goeth. Oh! do Thou forgive all our wanderings; do Thou strengthen us that in time to come we may live soberly, righteously, godly, and may less interrupt the flow of Thy friendship and love to us by our own departures from Thee. Surely it is true that none of them that trust in Thee shall be desolate. May we fulfill the condition, and do Thou fulfill the promise. For our Saviour Christ's sake. Amen.[2]

[2] From *Pulpit Prayers*.

THE RULE OF THE UNSEEN [1]

In proportion as our thoughts and desires are thus directed to things above, they will be averted from what is round about us; and the more longingly our eyes are fixed on the farthest horizon, the less shall we see flowers at our feet. To behold God pales the otherwise dazzling luster of created brightness. They whose souls are fed with heavenly manna, and who have learned that it is their necessary food, will scent no dainties in the fleshpots of Egypt, for all their rank garlic and leeks. It is simply a question as to which of two classes of ideas occupy the thoughts, and which of two sets of affections engage the heart.

If vulgar brawling and rude merrymaking fill the inn, there will be no room for the pilgrim thoughts which bear the Christ in their bosom, and have angels for their guard; and if these holy wayfarers enter, their serene presence will drive forth the noisy crowd, and turn the place into a temple.

If the unseen is ever to rule in men's lives, it must be through their thoughts. It must become intelligible, clear, real. Dreams and hopes, and peradventures are too unsubstantial stuff to be a bulwark against the very real, undeniable present. And such certitude is given through faith which grasps the promises of God, and twines the soul round the risen Saviour so closely that it sits with Him in heavenly places. Such certitude is given by faith alone.

[1] From *Similes and Figures from Alexander Maclaren,* by Francis E. Clark. Copyright, 1910, by Fleming H. Revell, and reprinted by permission.

7. MEMORY, HOPE, AND EFFORT [1]

"That they might set their hope in God, and not forget the works of God, but keep his commandments." Ps. 78:7.

In its original application this verse is simply a statement of God's purpose in giving to Israel the Law, and such a history of deliverance. The intention was that all future generations might remember what He had done, and be encouraged by the remembrance to hope in Him for the future; and, by both memory and hope, be impelled to the discharge of present duty.

So, then, the words may permissibly bear the application which I purpose to make of them in this sermon, re-echoing only (and aspiring to nothing more) the thoughts which the season has already, I suppose, more or less, suggested to most of us. Smooth motion is imperceptible; it is the jolts that tell us that we are advancing. Though every day be a New Year's Day, still the alteration in our dates and our calendars should set us all thinking of that continual lapse of the mysterious thing—the creature of our own minds—which we call Time, and which is bearing us all so steadily and silently onwards.

My text tells us how past, present, and future—memory, hope, and effort may be ennobled and blessed. In brief, it is by associating them all with God. It is as the field of His working that our past is best remembered. It is on Him that our hopes may most wisely be set. It is keeping His commandments which is the consecration of the present. Let us, then, take the three thoughts of our text and cast them into New Year's recommendations.

I. First, then, let us associate God with memory by thankful remembrance.

Now I suppose that there are very few of the faculties of our nature

[1] From *Christ's Musts*, Hodder & Stoughton Ltd. (London). Reprinted by permission.

which we more seldom try to regulate by Christian principles than that great power which we have of looking backwards. Did you ever reflect that you are responsible for what you remember, and for how you remember it, and that you are bound to train and educate your memory, not merely in the sense of cultivating it as a means of carrying intellectual treasures, but for a religious purpose? The one thing that all parts of our nature need is God, and that is as true about our power of remembrance as it is about any other part of our being. The past is then hallowed, noble, and yields its highest results and most blessed fruits for us when we link it closely with Him, and see in it not only, nor so much, the play of our own faculties, whether we blame or approve ourselves, as rather see in it the great field in which God has brought Himself near to our experience, and has been regulating and shaping all that has befallen us. The one thing which will consecrate memory, deliver it from its errors and abuses, raise it to its highest and noblest power, is that it should be in touch with God, and that the past should be regarded by each of us as it is, in deed and in truth, one long period of what God has done for us.

We can see His presence more clearly when we look back over a long connected stretch of days, and when the excitement of feeling the agony or rapture has passed, than we could whilst they were hot, and life was all hurry and bustle. The men on the deck of a ship see the beauty of the city that they have left behind, better than when they were pressing through its narrow streets. And though the view from the far-off waters of the receding houses may be an illusion, our view of the past, if we see God brooding over it all, and working in it all, is no illusion. The meannesses are hidden, the narrow places are invisible, all the pain and suffering is quieted, and we are able to behold more truly than when we were in the midst of it, the bearing, the purpose, and the blessedness alike of our sorrows and of our joys.

Many of us are old enough to have had a great many mysteries of our early days cleared up. We have seen at least the beginnings of the harvest which the ploughshare of sorrow and the winter winds were preparing for us, and for the rest we can trust. Brethren, remember your mercies; remember your losses; and "for all the way by which the Lord our God has led us these many years in the wilderness," let us try to be thankful, including in our praises the darkness and the storm as well as the light and the calm. Some of us are like people who, when they get better of their sicknesses, grudge the doctor's bill. We forget the mercies as soon as they are past, because we only enjoyed the sensuous sweetness of them whilst it tickled our palate, and did not think, in the enjoyment of them, whose love it was that they spoke of to us. Sorrows and joys, bring them all in your thanksgivings, and "forget not the works of God."

Such a habit of cultivating the remembrance of God's hand, moving in all our past, will not, in the slightest degree, interfere with lower and yet precious exercises of that same faculty. We shall still be able to look back, and learn our limitations, mark our weaknesses, gather counsels of prudence from our failures, tame our ambitions by remembering where we broke down. And such an exercise of grateful God-recognizing remembrance will deliver us from the abuses of that great power, by which so many of us turn our memories into a cause of weakness, if not of sin. There are people, and we are all tempted to be of the number, who look back upon the past and see nothing there but themselves, their own cleverness, their own success; burning incense to their own net, and sacrificing to their own drag. Another mood leads us to look back into the past dolefully and disappointedly, to say, "I have broken down so often; my resolutions have all gone to water so quickly; I have tried and failed over and over again. I may as well give it all up, and accept the inevitable, and grope on as well as I can without hope of self-advancement or of victory." Never! If only we will look back to God we shall be able to look forward to a perfect self. Tomorrow need never be determined by the failures that have been. We may still conquer where we have often been defeated. There is no worse use of the power of remembrance than when we use it to bind upon ourselves, as the permanent limitations of our progress, the failures and faults of the past. "Forget the things that are behind." Your old fragmentary goodness, your old foiled aspirations, your old frequent failures—cast them all behind you.

And there are others to whom remembrance is mainly a gloating over old sins, and a doing again of these—ruminating upon them; bringing up the chewed food once again to be masticated. Some of us gather only poisonous weeds, and carry them about in the *hortus siccus* of our memories. Alas! for the man whose memory is but the paler portraiture of past sins. Some of us, I am sure, have our former evils holding us so tight in their cords that when we look back memory is defiled by the things which defiled the unforgettable past. Brethren, you may find a refuge from that curse of remembrance in remembering God.

And some of us, unwisely and ungratefully, live in the light of departed blessings, so as to have no hearts either for present mercies or for present duties. There is no more weakening and foolish misdirection of that great gift of remembrance than when we employ it to tear down the tender greenery with which healing time has draped the ruins; or to turn again in the wound which is beginning to heal the sharp and poisoned point of the sorrow which once pierced it. For all these abuses—the memory that gloats upon sin; the memory that is proud of success; the memory that is despondent because of failures; the memory that is tearful and brokenhearted over losses—for all these the remedy is that we should not forget the works of God, but see Him everywhere filling the past.

II. Again, let us live in the future by hope in Him.

Our remembrances and our hopes are closely connected; one might almost even say that the power by which we look backwards and that by which we look forwards are one and the same. At all events, Hope owes to Memory the pigments with which it paints, the canvas on which it paints, and the objects which it portrays there. But in all our earthly hopes there is a feeling of uncertainty which brings alarm as well as expectation. And he whose forward vision runs only along the low levels of earth, and is fed only by experience and remembrance, will never be able to say, "I hope with certitude, and I know that my hope shall be fulfilled." For him "hopes, and fears that kindle hopes," will be "an indistinguishable throng"; and there will be as much of pain as of pleasure in his forward glance.

But if, according to my text, we set our hopes on God, then we shall have a certainty absolute. What a blessing it is to be able to look forward to a future as fixed and as sure, as solid and as real, as much our possession as the irrevocable past! The Christian man's hope, if it be set on God, is not a "may be," but a "will be"; and he can be as sure of tomorrow as he is of yesterday.

They whose hopes are set on God have a certain hope, a sufficient one, and one that fills all the future. All other expectations are fulfilled or disappointed, as the case may be, but are left behind and outgrown. This one only never palls, and is never accomplished, and yet is never disappointed. So if we set our hopes on Him, we can face very quietly the darkness that lies ahead of us. Earthly hopes are only the mirrors in which the past reflects itself, as in some king's palace you will find a lighted chamber, with a great sheet of glass at each end, which perpetuates in shining rows the lights behind the spectator. A curtain veils the future, and earthly hope can only put a mirror in front of it that reflects what has been. But the hope that is set on God draws back the curtain, and lets us see enough of a fixed, eternal future to make our lives bright and our hearts calm. The darkness remains; what of that, if "I know I shall not drift beyond His love and care"? Set your hopes on God, and they will not be ashamed.

III. Lastly, let us live in the present by strenuous obedience.

After all, memory and hope are meant to fit us for work in the flying moment. Both should impel us to this keeping of the commandments of God; for both yield motives which should incline us thereto. A past full of blessing demands the sacrifice of loving hearts and of earnest hands. A future so fair, so far, so certain, so sovereign, and a hope that grasps it, and brings some of its sweet fragrance into the else scentless air of the poor present, ought to impel to service, vigorous and continual. Both should yield motives which make such service a delight.

If my memory weakens me for present work, either because it depresses my hope of success, or because it saddens me with the remembrance of departed blessings, then it is a curse and not a good. And if I dream myself away in any future, and forget the exigencies of the imperative and swiftly-passing moment, then the faculty of hope, too, is a curse and a weakening. But both are delivered from their possible abuses, if both are made into means of helping us to fill the present with loving obedience. These two faculties are like the two wings that may lift us to God, like the two paddles, one on either side of the ship, that may drive on steadily forward, through all the surges and the tempest. These find their highest field in fitting us for the grinding tasks and the heavy burdens that the moment lays upon us.

So, dear friends, we are very different in our circumstances and positions. For some of us Hope's basket is nearly empty, and Memory's sack is very full. For us older men the past is long, the earthly future is short. For you younger people the converse is the case. It is Hope whose hands are laden with treasures for you. Memory carries but a little store. Your past is brief; your future is probably long. The grains of sand in some of our hour glasses are very heaped and high in the lower half, and running very low in the upper. But whichever category we stand in, one thing remains the same for us all, and that is duty, keeping God's commandments. That is permanent, and that is the one thing worth living for. "Whether we live we live unto the Lord; or whether we die we die unto the Lord."

So let us front this New Year, with all its hidden possibilities, with quiet, brave hearts, resolved on present duty, as those ought who have such a past to remember and such a future to hope for. It will probably be the last on earth for some of us. It will probably contain great sorrows for some of us, and great joys for others. It will probably be comparatively uneventful for others. It may make great outward changes for us, or it may leave us much as it found us. But, at all events, God will be in it, and work for Him should be in it. Well for us if, when its hours have slidden away into the grey past, they continue to witness to us of His love, even as, while they were wrapped in the mists of the future, they called on us to hope in Him! Well for us if we fill the passing moment with deeds of loving obedience! Then a present of keeping His commandments will glide into a past to be thankfully remembered, and will bring us nearer to a future in which hope shall not be put to shame. To him who sees God in all the divisions and particles of his days, and makes Him the object of memory, hope, and effort, past, present, and future are but successive calm ripples of that mighty river of Time which bears him on the great ocean of Eternity, from which the drops that make its waters rose, and to which its ceaseless flow returns.

O Lord! our Helper and our Home, we would come to Thee again this morning, and draw near to that Presence which we have often found to be full of light and joy and peace and power.

Look upon us, we pray Thee, gathered here before Thee now. We thank Thee for all the mercies which have led us up into Thy house today. We bless Thee for the assurance of still greater benefits which meets us when we gather together thus, and lift up our hearts to Thee. We pray that Thou wouldst reveal to each waiting heart the fullness of Thy love, and the power of Thy presence.

To all the solitary draw near as the Companion that makes up for the absence of all beside. For any that are in perplexity do Thou disclose Thy purposes and their path. Strengthen us for all our work; lay upon hearts and consciences the clear vision of our duties, and make us willing to accept and to discharge them. May we find Thee waiting for us in all the various departments of our lives. And may all our work, of whatever sort it is, be offered up to Thee, and by Thee be furthered and prospered. "Day unto day uttereth speech, and night unto night showeth knowledge." For all Thy loving-kindness, Thy deep and wise providence, Thy tender care, receive our praise. And may we never leave Thy mercies forgotten, nor waste them by unfaithful reception of Thy great goodnesses. Through Jesus Christ our Lord and Saviour. Amen.[2]

---

[2] From *Pulpit Prayers*.

ENVELOPING LOVE [1]

And that love which thus towers above us, and gleams like the shining cross on the top of some lofty cathedral spire, does not flash up there inaccessibly, nor lie before us like some pathless precipice, up which nothing that has not wings can ever hope to rise, but the height of the love of Christ is an hospitable height, which can be scaled by us.

Nay, rather, that heaven of love which is "higher than our thoughts," bends down, as by a kind of optical delusion the physical heaven seems to do, towards each of us, only with this blessed difference, that in the natural world the place where heaven touches earth is always the furthest point of distance from us; and in the spiritual world, the place where heaven stoops to me is always right over my head, and the nearest possible point to me. He has come to lift us to Himself. And this is the height of His love, that it bears us up, if we will, up and up to sit upon that throne where He Himself is enthroned.

But remember, this ocean of love you can shut out of your lives. It is possible to plunge a jar into mid-Atlantic, further than soundings have ever descended, and to bring it up on deck as dry inside as if it had been lying on an oven. It is possible for men and women to live and move and have their being in that sea of love, and never to have let one drop of its richest gifts into their hearts or their lives. Open your hearts for Him to come in, by humble faith in His sacrifice for you.

---

[1] From *Similes and Figures from Alexander Maclaren*, by Francis E. Clark. Copyright, 1910, by Fleming H. Revell, and reprinted by permission.

8. A SONG OF FAITH [1]

"He that dwelleth in the secret place of the Most High shall abide under the shadow of the Almighty." Ps. 91:1.

I have read this verse, but I desire to deal, not with it merely, but with the whole of the psalm, of which it is the introduction. The one theme of it is the security and absolute immunity from mortal ills, which belong to those that dwell in God. That one thought is worked out with wonderful force and variety. The singer is borne aloft on the two wings of devout confidence and poetic imagination, and when these two beat in unison, they lift a man high. If we try to follow him as he soars, perhaps we too, in some measure, may be raised above the cares and sorrows of this low-thoughted earth.

One preliminary remark I must make, and that is, that throughout the psalm there is a very remarkable alternation of speakers. It begins with, "*I* will say of the Lord"; there immediately follows, "*He* shall deliver thee"; and so on. And at the end, the person who had spoken first as "I," and been spoken *to* as "thou" and "thee," is spoken *of* by yet another voice, which says, "He has set His love upon me." That remarkable and dramatic alternation of speakers is yet more conspicuous in the original than it appears in our Authorized Version, because, imbedded in the very middle of that second portion, in which "thou" is the prevailing word, we have a verse which, as it stands in the Authorized Version, is bewildering, and scarcely intelligible without a great deal of ekeing out—"because thou hast made the Lord, which is my Refuge, even the Most High, thy habitation." We get lost amidst the "mys" and the "thys," but the Revised Version, following the original, clears the matter up, for it reads thus: "Thou, Lord, art my Refuge." There speaks the first voice, coming in again with its "my," and then the second voice once more

---

[1] From *Last Sheaves*, American Tract Society, 1904. Reprinted by permission.

responds: "Thou hast made the Lord thy habitation, there shall no evil befall thee." So twice we have the solitary profession of personal faith, twice responded to by a stream of great assurances, and these are finally confirmed and enlarged by the voice of God Himself.

First, then, we have here

I. The solitary voice of faith.

The words that I have read as my text, which stand as the introduction to the psalm, are the expression in the most general form of that great truth which it is all intended to enforce and to illustrate. They are chosen with exquisite beauty and felicity: "He that dwelleth in the secret place of the Most High"—how high up that "secret place" must be! how deep the silence up there! how pure the air! How far above the poisonous mists that cling to the low-lying swamps, how far out of the reach of the arrows or shots of the foeman is he that dwelleth with God by communion, by constancy of desire, by aspiration, and by clear recognition of the Divine goal of all his efforts in the midst of his most strenuous and distracting work, and his most crushing and exhausting sorrows! "He that dwelleth" thus, "in the secret place of the Most High, shall abide under the shadow of the Almighty"—and since He is Almighty, the long shadow that that great rock casts will shelter him who keeps beneath it from the burning rays of the fiery sunshine, in every "weary land." The plain English of the highly imaginative words is, Let me keep myself in touch with God, and I keep myself master of all things, and secure from the evil that is in evil.

That is the general truth, but religious commonplaces lose their power by their generality, and in order to give them force we must point them to a personal application. So the psalmist, encouraged by his contemplation of that broad universal principle, takes it for his own, and brings "I" and "my" into it, and that changes it from a toothless, useless, threadbare commonplace, which a man may have in his creed without its doing him one morsel of good, into a living experience. "*I* will say of the Lord, He is *my* Rock and *my* Fortress; *my* God, in Whom *I* will trust." Do *we* say that? Have we translated the universal into the particular? Has the contemplation of the most wide-stretching truth encouraged us to grasp it and make it our very own? To do so gives gloss to the threadbare, freshness to the trite and familiar, beauty and force to the commonplace. And there is no religion which is not the appropriation to my very own self of the great truths that are meant for the world. So much of Niagara as you turn into your own sluice will irrigate your barren fields and slake your thirst, and all the rest, as far as you are concerned, is waste. It is useless to say, however solemnly, and with however entire assent of the understanding, "he that dwelleth in the secret place of the Most High shall abide under the shadow of the Almighty"—unless you take the further step, and in your own needs and sorrows, in your own hours of weakness and of stress when the enemy is coming in like a flood, say "*my* Fortress, *my* Strength, *my* God in Whom *I* will trust."

Next we come to

II. The great assurances which answer to this solitary voice of faith.

Whether the psalm was intended to be sung by any kind of alternate responsive choir and solo voices or no, we need not consider; at all events, it is laid out in that structure which I have already pointed out. So when the single soul has brought itself up, by the effort of its faith, to make God its Refuge and its Fortress, then there come pouring in upon it, as if spoken from without, but yet brought near to it and made audible for it by its own personal faith, a whole host of great certainties.

"Surely he shall deliver thee from the snare of the fowler, and from the noisome pestilence." The "fowler" is in other places of Scripture taken as a metaphor for death; and obviously the thing that was chiefly, if not exclusively, in the psalmist's mind here, was the assurance of protection from insidious threatening evils that affected physical life. The "pestilence" and the "fowler" stand for these.

Then there follows a beautiful description of the manner and condition of that Divine protection: "He shall cover thee with his feathers." That carries us back to the old word about the eagle stirring up its nest, and bearing its young upon its pinions, and suggests the tenderness that is lodged in the might of that Divine nature; and how He, the loftiest, knows what it is to have paternal care over them that put their trust in Him. But we must not forget a yet more gracious expansion of the word when, in the course of ages, One caught up the echoes of the old, sweet metaphor, and said: "As a hen gathereth her chickens under her wings," so I would have gathered thee. Christ turned away from the emblem of the fierce bird of prey, and with lowly love, took up the emblem of the harmless domestic fowl to express the warmth, the security, of the relation of the loving servant to the Master-Lord.

But, further, we have to note that there is here, too, the condition on which the shelter of that strong pinion is ours. "He shall cover thee with his feathers," but not unless "Under his wings shalt thou trust," or, as the word had better be rendered in this connection, "Under his wings shalt thou flee for refuge." What becomes of the chickens that are straying about the barnyard, when kites are in the sky or the fox lurking behind the wall? They are snapped up. What becomes of the Christian man that strays out of the protection of the covering wing, and by self-will, or failure of trust, or practical disobedience, or fixing the heart and desire on earthly things, gets away from his Defense and his Defender? What becomes of him? The snare of the fowler is not spread in vain, and he is caught and limed there. If you want to be guarded by Jesus, keep your hearts and minds close to Jesus. Further, the ground of security is laid, not in our faith, but in His faithfulness. "His truth"—that is to say, to use the old word which expresses the idea much better, "His truth —shall be thy shield and buckler." The ground of our conscious security is laid in His faithfulness to all His promises.

Now is all this true? Is it true, as the psalmist goes on to portray under the double figure of battle and pestilence, that the man who thus trusts is saved from widespread calamities, which may be devastating the lives of a community? If we look on the surface it is not true. Those that "dwell in the secret place of the Most High" will die of an epidemic, cholera, or smallpox, like the men beside them, that have no such abode. *Our* hearts have often risen in protest against such promises as this of my text, when those that have been "dwelling in the secret place of the Most High" have been stealthily snared and swept away from us. But, for all that, brethren, it is true; it is true. For suppose two men, one a Christian, another not, both of them suffering from the same epidemic, both of them dying from it. Yet the difference between the two is such as that we may confidently say of the one, "He that believeth shall never die," and of the other that he has died. It is irrelevant to talk about vaccination being a better prophylactic than faith. No doubt this psalmist was thinking mainly of physical life. No doubt, also, you and I have better means of interpreting and understanding Providence and its dealings, than he had, and for us the belief that they who "dwell in the secret place of the Most High" are immune from death, is possible and imperative, after a fashion far nobler and better than the psalmist could have dreamed.

I need point out to you how here, beautifully and picturesquely, the two metaphors of battle and disease are each parted into their two halves, one expressive of open, and the other of secret, assaults—"the pestilence that walketh in darkness" on the one hand, "the destruction that wasteth at noonday" on the other; "the terror by night," of nocturnal assaults upon a defenseless camp, on the one hand, and "the arrow that flieth by day," on the other. Only let us take this to heart, that all manner of danger and assaults are included in the promise, and though sense seems to say that the promise is but as gossamer seen by moonlight, a beautiful dream with no substance in it; yet a deeper perception of the reality of things tells us that to the hilt it is fulfilled, and that they who dwell in God shall never see death.

There follows, according to the rendering which I have already given, the glad "Yes" of the solitary soul. "For Thou, Lord, art my Refuge." That utterance of faith is even more condensed than was the former. As we have seen, the initial utterance of trust brought to the psalmist's consciousness the great and glorious promises of which I have been speaking. When they come into his consciousness, then the office of his faith is to grasp them. He has only the cheque, only the draft; but it is as good to him as bullion. "For," says he—and note that "for"—"Thou, Lord, art my Refuge." That is to say, he listens to all the preceding promises, and smiles and says, "Yes, I know it is all true; because Thou art my Refuge." And when he says that he is thinking both of God's character and of his own faith. Thou art my Refuge in Thyself, and because I have chosen Thee to be so. When there come into our hearts and minds, in sequence to some poor utterances of our faith, perhaps in an hour when our hearts are very sore and our lives very dark, these great assurances of a present God and an immortal life, let us be sure that our faith further rises to grasp, and say Amen to, them, rooting itself in the assurance of what God is, and of what we have chosen Him to be. Samuel Rutherford says that God's promises are like the boughs of a tree bending over a river, for His half-drowned children to lay hold of. Let us see that, when they are suggested to our faith, our faith grasps them.

There follows a series of further promises, even greater than those that have preceded. "There shall no evil befall thee, neither shall any plague come nigh thy dwelling," or, as it reads in the original "thy tent," suggesting the nomad life. We have two houses; a shifting tent, the frail structure of our earthly habitation, and a "house not made with hands, eternal in the heavens," which is God Himself. "Because thou hast made the Most High thy habitation there shall no evil . . . come nigh thy dwelling." If thou dwell in God thou dwellest in safety.

Then there follow other promises which regard the nomad, not as in his tent, but, as on the road; promises that he shall be kept in all his ways, promises that he shall not only be kept in his ways, but that on angel's hands he shall be lifted buoyant and safe over his difficulties, and promises still greater than these, that in his conflict he shall be victor, and "shall tread upon the lion and the adder." There again we have the antithesis of open and secret hostility. In these promises of keeping in the active life, of buoying over difficulties and of victory over enemies, we have more than the preceding promises of immunity from danger. We are here on the verge of promises as to spiritual necessities and conflicts, and are being assured that "he that dwelleth in the secret place of the Most High" may continue there, and yet be trudging along the rough road of life; and that, if we thus combine the inward peace of communion, and the effort of active life, we shall "be kept in our ways," and upheld in our ways, and have victory over the lurking foes that would wound our heel, and the open enemies that would rend our life.

We must remember Old Testament conditions when we read Old Testament promises, and we must apply New Testament interpretations to Old Testament assurances. When we read, "There shall no evil befall thee," and think of our own harassed, tempest-tossed, often sorrowful lives, and broken, solitary hearts, we must learn that the evil that educates is not evil, and that the chastening of the Father's hand is good; and that nothing that brings a man nearer to God can be his enemy. The poison is wiped off the arrow, though the arrow may mercifully wound; and the evil in the evil is all dissipated.

Lastly, we have

III. A deeper voice still, coming in, confirming and enlarging all these promises.

I can but gather up these final utterances in a few words. God Himself speaks, promising deliverance consequent upon fixed love. "Because he hath set his love upon me, therefore will I deliver him." He is not going to fail in response to the love of His child's heart. As the word in the original suggests, when a poor man presses himself close up against the Divine breast, as a dog might against his master's limbs, or as one that loves might clasp close to himself the beloved, then God responds to the desire for close contact, and through such contact He brings deliverance.

Further, that Divine Voice promises elevation consequent on acquaintance with the Divine Character. "I will set him on high"—high above all the weltering flood of evil, that washes vainly round the base of the cliff—"because he hath known my name." Loving acquaintance with the revealed character of God lifts a man above earth and all its ills.

Further, there is the promise of Divine companionship consequent on sorrows. "I will be with him in trouble." Some of us know what that means, how we never got a glimpse of God until earth was dark, and how when a devastating flood, as it seemed, came sweeping over the fair gardens of our lives, we found, when it had gone back, that it had left fertility such as we had never before been capable of. Night brings the darkness, and darkness brings the stars. Trouble rightly borne brings God, and any flood that bears Him into my soul, can be only a flood of blessing.

"With long life will I satisfy him, and show him my salvation." Again I say, bring New Testament interpretation to Old Testament promises, for the evolution of God's revelation of His will makes it wise to interpret the imperfect by the complete. "With long life will I satisfy him," through the ages of eternity, and "show him my salvation" in the glories of an immortal life. Brethren, let us keep the conditions. Let us set our love on Him, know His will, call upon Him and listen for His answer, dwell in the secret place of the Most High, and He will fulfill His promises, then no evil shall befall us, but our earthly life will be filled with good, and will lead on to the more perfect manifestations of His saving power through the ages of eternity.

O Lord, Who art Thyself the ever-blessed God, and with Whom are joys unspeakable and full of glory, grant, we beseech Thee, to each of us a portion in that changeless blessedness and deep tranquil gladness which comes to those who live in and near Thee.

Look upon us all gathered here before Thee. Thou! O Lord, knowest our needs, our characters, the motives that have brought us together, the spirit in which we have come, the expectations that we have cherished. If these are unworthy, forgive them; if they are good, satisfy them.

If any of us are in any special circumstances or difficulties, do Thou keep our feet, though they be in slippery places; and do Thou help us to realize, at all times and places, Thy presence, not as if in the sight of a tyrant Taskmaster, but as under the loving observation of a gracious Father. And may the remembrance of Thy presence, and the confidence of Thy help, minister strength and steadfastness to us. We would leave ourselves in Thy hands, and pray Thee to help us, day by day, to live noble, worthy, self-sacrificing, and Christlike lives, by the power of the great Saviour in Whom alone we desire to trust. Amen.[2]

---

[2] From *Pulpit Prayers*.

TODAY AND TOMORROW [1]

Today's wealth may be tomorrow's poverty, today's health tomorrow's sickness, today's happy companionship of love tomorrow's aching solitude of heart, but today's God will be tomorrow's God, today's Christ will be tomorrow's Christ. Other fountains may dry up in heat or freeze in winter, but this knows no change; "in summer and winter it shall be." Other fountains may sink low in their basins after much drawing, but this is ever full, and, after a thousand generations have drawn from its stream, is broad and deep as ever.

Other fountains may be left behind on the march, and the wells and palm trees of each Elim on our road be succeeded by a dry and thirsty land where no water is, but this spring follows us all through the wilderness, and makes music, and spreads freshness ever by our path. We can forecast nothing beside. We can be sure of this, that God will be with us in all the days that lie before us. What may be round the next headland we know not; but this we know, that the same sunshine will make a broadening path across the waters right to where we rock on the unknown sea, and the same unmoving mighty star will burn for our guidance.

[1] From *Similes and Figures from Alexander Maclaren*, by Francis E. Clark. Copyright, 1910, by Fleming H. Revell, and reprinted by permission.

9. CHRIST'S MUSTS [1]

"Even so must the Son of man be lifted up." JOHN 3:14.

I have chosen this text for the sake of one word in it, that solemn "must" which was so often on our Lord's lips. I have no purpose of dealing with the remainder of this clause, nor, indeed, with it at all, except as one instance of His use of the expression. But I felt it might be interesting, and might set old truths in a brighter light, if we gather together the instances in which Christ speaks of the great necessity which dominated His life, and shaped even small acts.

The expression is most frequently used in reference to the Passion and Resurrection. There are many instances in the other Gospels, in which He speaks of that *must*. The first of these is that of my text. Then there is another class, of which His word to His mother when a twelve-year-old child may be taken as a type, "Wist ye not that I *must* be about my Father's business?" where the mysterious consciousness of a special relation to God in the child's heart drew Him to the Temple, and to His Father's work. Other similar instances are those in which He responded to the multitude when they wanted to keep Him to themselves: "I *must* preach in other cities also"; or, as when He said, "I *must* work the works of him that sent me while it is day."

Yet another aspect of the same necessity is presented when, looking far beyond the earthly work and suffering, He discerned the future triumph which was to be the issue of these, and said, "Other sheep I have . . . them also I *must* bring."

And yet another is in reference to a very small matter: His selection of a place for a few hours' rest on His last fateful journey to Jerusalem, when He said, "Zaccheus, . . . today I must abide at thy house."

---
[1] From *Christ's Musts*, Hodder & Stoughton Ltd. (London). Reprinted by permission.

Now, if we put these instances together, we shall get some precious glimpses into our Lord's heart and His view of life.

I. Here we see Christ recognizing and accepting the necessity for His death.

My text, if we accept John's Gospel, contributes an altogether new element to our conception of our Lord as announcing His death. For the other three Gospels lay emphasis on it as being part of His teaching, especially during the latter stage of His ministry. But it does not follow that He began to think about it or to see it, when He began to speak about it. There are reasons for the earlier comparative reticence, and there is no ground for the conclusion that then first began to dawn upon a disappointed enthusiast the grim reality that His work was not going to prosper, and that martyrdom was necessary. That is a notion that has been frequently upheld of late years, but to me it seems altogether incongruous with the facts of the case. And, if John's Gospel is a true record, that theory is shivered against this text, which represents Him at the very beginning of His career—the time when, according to that other theory, He was full of the usual buoyant and baseless anticipations of a reformer commencing His course—as telling Nicodemus, "Even so must the Son of man be lifted up." In like manner, in the previous chapter of this same Gospel, we have the significant though enigmatical utterance: "Destroy this temple, and in three days I will raise it up"; with the Evangelist's authoritative comment: "He spake of the temple of his body." So, from the beginning of His career, the end was clear before Him.

And why *must* He go to the Cross? Not merely, as the other evangelists put it, in order that "it might be fulfilled which was spoken by the prophets." It was not that Jesus must die because the prophets had said that Messiah should, but that the prophets had said that Messiah should because Jesus must. There was a far deeper necessity than the fulfillment of any prophetic utterance, even the necessity which shaped that utterance. The work of Jesus Christ could not be done unless He died. He could not be the Saviour of the world unless He was the sacrifice for the sins of the world.

We cannot see all the grounds of that solemn imperative, but this we can see, that it was because of the requirements of the divine righteousness, and because of the necessities of sinful men. And so Christ's was no martyr's death, who had to die as the penalty of the faithful discharge of his duty. It was not the penalty that He paid for doing His work, but it was the work itself. Not that gracious life, not "the loveliness of perfect deeds," nor His words of sweet wisdom, nor His acts of transcendent power, equaled only by the pity that moved the power, completed His task, but He came "to give his life a ransom for many."

"Must" is a hard word. It may express an unwelcome necessity. Was this necessity unwelcome? When He said: "The Son of Man must be lifted up," was He shrinking, or reluctantly submitting? Ah, no! He *must* die because He *would* save, and He *would* save because He *did* love. His filial obedience to God coincided with His pity for men; and not merely in obedience to the requirements of the Divine righteousness, but in compassion for the necessities of sinners, necessity was laid upon Him.

Oh, brethren nothing held Christ to the Cross but His own desire to save us. Neither priests nor Romans carried Him thither. What fastened Him to it was not the nails driven by rude hands. And the reason why He did not, as the taunters bade Him do, come down from it, was neither a physical nor a moral necessity unwelcome to Himself, but the yielding of His own will to do all which was needed for man's salvation.

This Sacrifice was bound to the altar by the cords of love. We have heard of martyrs who have refused to be tied to the stake, and have kept themselves motionless in the center of the fierce flames by the force of their wills. Jesus Christ fastened Himself to the Cross and died because He would.

And, oh! if we think of that sweet, serene life as having clear before it from the very first steps that grim end, how infinitely it gains in pathetic beauty and in heart-touchingness! What wonderful self-abnegation! How He was at leisure from Himself, with a heart of pity for every sorrow, and loins girt for all service, though for all His life the Cross closed the vista! Think! human shrinking was felt by Him. Think! it was so held back that His purpose never faltered. Think! each of us may say, "He *must* die because He *would* save me"; and then ask, "What shall I render unto the Lord for all his benefits toward me?"

II. In a second class of these utterances, we see Christ impelled by filial obedience and the consciousness of His mission.

"Wist ye not that I must be about my Father's business?" That was a strange utterance for a boy of twelve. It seems to negative the supposition that what is called the "Messianic consciousness" dawned upon Jesus Christ first after His baptism and the descent of the Spirit. But however that may be, it and the similar passages to which I have already referred, bearing upon His discharge of His work prior to His death, teach that the necessity was an inward necessity springing from His consciousness of Sonship, and His recognition of the work that He had to do. And so He is our great Example of spontaneous obedience, which does violence to itself if it does not obey. It was instinct that sent the boy into the Temple. Where should a son be but in His Father's house? How could He not be doing His Father's business?

Thus He stands before us, the pattern for the only obedience that is worth calling so, the obedience which would be pained and ill at ease unless it were doing the work of God. Religion is meant to make it a second nature, or, as I have ventured to call it, an instinct—a spontaneous, uncalculating, irrepressible desire—to be in fellowship with God, and to be doing His will. That is the meaning of our Christianity. There is no obedience in reluctant obedience; forced service is slavery, not service. Christianity is given for the specific purpose that it may bring us so into touch with Jesus Christ as that the mind which was in Him may be in us; and we too may be able to say, with a kind of wonder that people should have expected to find us in any other place, or doing anything else, "Wist ye not that because I am a son, I must be about my Father's business?" As certainly as the sunflower follows the sun, so certainly will a man, animated by the mind that was in Jesus Christ, like Him find his very life's breath in doing the Father's will.

So then, brethren, what about our grudging service? What about our reluctant obedience? What about the widespread mistake that religion prohibits wished-for things and enforces unwelcome duties? If my Christianity does not make me recoil from what it forbids, and spring eagerly to what it commends, my Christianity is of very little use. If when in the temple we are like idle boys in school, always casting glances at the clock and the door, and wishing ourselves outside, we may just as well be out as in. Glad obedience is true obedience. Only he who can say, "Thy law is within my heart, and I do Thy will because I love Thee, and cannot but do as Thou desirest," has found the joy possible to a Christian life. It is not "harsh and crabbed," as those that look upon it from the outside may suppose, but musical and full of sweetness. There is nothing more blessed than when "I choose" covers exactly the same ground as "I ought." And when duty is delight, delight will never become disgust, nor joy pass away.

III. We see, in yet another use of this great "must," Christ anticipating His future triumph.

"Other sheep I have, which are not of this fold: them also I must bring . . . and there shall be one flock and one shepherd." Striking as these words are in themselves, they are still more striking when we notice their connection; for they follow immediately upon His utterance about laying down His life for the sheep. So, then, His work was beyond the cross. And whatever it was, it was to be done after He had died.

I need not point out to you how far afield Christ's vision goes out into the dim, waste places, where on the dark mountains the straying sheep are torn and frightened and starving. I need not dwell upon how far ahead in the future His glance travels, or how magnificent and how rebuking to our petty narrowness the great word is. "There shall be one *flock*" (not fold); and they shall be one, not because they are within the bounds of any visible "fold," but because they are gathered round the one Shepherd, and in their common relation to Him are knit together in unity.

But what sort of Man is this who considers that His widest work is to be done by Him after He is dead? "Them also I *must* bring." Thou! How? When? Surely such words as these, side by side with the clear prevision of the death that was so soon to come, are either meaningless or the utterance of an arrogance bordering on insanity; or they anticipate what an evangelist declares did take place—that the Lord was taken up into heaven and sat at the right hand of God, whilst His servants went everywhere preaching the Word, the Lord also working with them and "confirming the word" with the signs He wrought.

"Them also I must bring." That is not merely a necessity rooted in the nature of God and the wants of men. It is not merely a necessity springing from Christ's filial obedience and sense of a mission; but it is a "must" of destiny, a "must" which recognizes the sure results of His passion; a "must" which implies the power of the Cross to be the reconciliation of the world. And so for all pessimistic thoughts today, or at any time, and when Christian men's hearts may be trembling for the Ark of God—although, perhaps, there may be little reason for the tremor—and in the face of all blatant antagonisms and of proud Goliaths despising the "foolishness of preaching," we fall back upon Christ's great "must." It is written in the councils of Heaven more unchangeably than the heavens; it is guaranteed by the power of the Cross; it is certain, by the eternal life of the crucified Saviour, that He will one day be the King of humanity, and *must* bring His wandering sheep to couch in peace, one flock round one Shepherd.

IV. Lastly, we have Christ applying the greatest principle to the smallest duty.

"Zaccheus, make haste, and come down; today I *must* abide in thy house." Why must He? Because Zaccheus was to be saved, and was worth saving. What was the "must"? To stop for an hour or two on His road to the Cross. So He teaches us that in a life penetrated by the thought of the Divine will, which we gladly obey, there are no things too great, and none too trivial, to be brought under the dominion of that law, and to be regulated by that Divine necessity. Obedience is obedience, whether in large things or in small. There is no scale of magnitude applicable to the distinction between God's will and that which is not God's will. Gravitation rules the motes that dance in the sunshine as well as the mass of Jupiter. A triangle with its apex in the sun, and its base beyond the solar system, has the same properties and comes under the same laws as one that a schoolboy scrawls upon his slate. God's truth is not too great to rule the smallest duties. The star in the east was a guide to the humble house at Bethlehem, and there are starry truths high in the heavens that avail for our guidance in the smallest acts of life.

So, brethren, bring your doing under that all-embracing law of duty —duty, which is the heathen expression for the will of God. There are great regions of life in which lower necessities have play. Circumstances, our past, bias and temper, relationship, friendship, civic duty, and the like—all these bring their necessities; but let us think of them all as being, what indeed they are, manifestations to us of the will of our Father. There are great tracts of life in which either of two courses may be right, and we are left to the decision of choice rather than of duty; but high above all these, let us see towering that Divine necessity. It is a daily struggle to bring "I will" to coincide with "I ought"; and there is only one adequate and always powerful way of securing that coincidence, and it is to keep close to Jesus Christ and to drink in His spirit. Then, when duty and delight are conterminous, the rough places will be plain, and the crooked things straight, and every mountain shall be brought low, and every valley shall be exalted, and life will be blessed, and service will be freedom. Joy and liberty and power and peace will fill our hearts when this is the law of our being: "All that the Lord hath spoken, that *must* I do."

Almighty and most loving Father! We bow before that "mighty" and "vast" command, and we draw near to that inexhaustible love, and beseech Thee that our fleeting being may be built on "the Rock" of Ages, and so stand fast, like Thine, "When rolling years shall cease to move." Blessed be Thy name, we can come to Thee, Eternal and All-loving; and though we are the creatures of a day, we can share in the years which are throughout all generations. May none of us here live only for the things seen and temporal, but all of us have eyes cleared so as to behold and walk in the light of the things unseen and eternal.

Look upon us as we are gathered in Thy presence now. Help us in our worship. May our thoughts be fixed on Thee, and our desires go out after Thee. Help us in hearing and in speaking Thy word; and let all unfitness, whether of body or of mind, be taken away by Thy gracious coming to us; that in this hour every one of us may feel that God Himself draws near to us, and that the voice of each of us may be, "Speak, Lord; for Thy servant heareth."

We beseech Thee to answer us now, and to give us the rejoicing sense of Thy presence and love, that our worship may be glad, inspiring, quickening, and complete, through Jesus Christ our Saviour. Amen.[2]

[2] From *Pulpit Prayers*

THE MATTER OF A DAY IN ITS DAY [1]

That little word "grace" is like a small window that opens out on to a great landscape, for it gathers up into one encyclopedical expression the whole infinite variety of beneficences and bestowments which come showering down upon us. That one gift is, as the Apostle puts it in one of his eloquent epithets, "the manifold *grace of God," which word in the original is even more rich and picturesque, because it means the "many-variegated grace," like some rich piece of embroidery glowing with all manner of dyes and gold. So the one gift comes to us manifold, rich in its adaption to and its exquisite fitness for, the needs of the moment. God's gift comes to us with like variety, the "matter of a day in its day."*

Am I struggling? He extends a hand to steady me. Am I fighting? He is my sword and shield, "my buckler, and the horn of my salvation, and my high tower." Am I anxious? He comes into my heart, and brings with Him a great peace, and all waves cease to toss, and smooth themselves into a level plain. There is One by my side who will neither change nor fail nor die. Whatever any man needs, at the moment that he needs it, that one great Gift shall supply the "matter of a day in its day."

[1] From *Similes and Figures from Alexander Maclaren,* by Francis E. Clark. Copyright, 1910, by Fleming H. Revell, and reprinted by permission.

10. THE SHELTERING WING [1]

"He shall cover thee with his feathers, and under his wings shalt thou trust: his truth shall be thy shield and buckler." Ps. 91:4.

I was recently speaking from the magnificent image in Moses' song, of God's protection and guidance as that of the eagle who stirred up his nest, and hovered over the young with his wings, and bore them on his pinions. That passage has led my thoughts to this one, in which the same general metaphor is employed, but with a distinct and significant difference in its application. In the former image the main idea, as I tried to show, is that of training and sustaining. Here the main idea is that of protection and fostering. *On* the wing and *under* the wing suggest entirely different notions, and both need to be taken into account in order to get the many-sided beauties and promises of these great sayings. Now, there seems to me here to be a very distinct triad of thoughts. There is the covering wing; there is the flight to its protection; and there is the warrant for that flight. "He shall cover thee with His pinions"; that is the Divine act. "Under His wings shalt thou trust"; that is the human condition. "His truth shall be thy shield and buckler"; that is the Divine manifestation which makes the human condition possible.

I. A word, then, first about the covering wing.

Now, the main idea in this image is, as I have suggested, that of the expanded pinion, beneath the shelter of which the callow young lie and are guarded. Whatsoever kites may be in the sky, whatsoever stoats and weasels may be in the hedges, they are safe there. The images suggests not only the thought of protection but those of fostering, downy warmth, peaceful proximity to a heart that throbs with parental love, and a multitude of other happy privileges realized by those who nestle

[1] From *Triumphant Certainties,* American Baptist Publication Society, 1897.

beneath that wing. But while these subsidiary ideas are not to be lost sight of, the promise of protection is to be kept clear, as that chiefly intended by the psalmist.

This psalm rings throughout with the doctrine that a man who dwells "in the secret place of the Most High" has absolute immunity from all sorts of evil; and there are two regions in which that immunity, secured by being under the shadow of the Almighty, is exemplified in the psalm. The one is that of outward dangers, the other is that of temptation to sin and what we may call spiritual foes. Now, these two regions and departments in which the Christian man does realize, in the measure of his faith, the Divine protection, exhibit that protection as administered in two entirely different ways.

The triumphant assurances of this psalm—"There shall no evil befall thee, neither shall any plague come nigh thy dwelling," "The pestilence shall smite thousands and ten thousands beside thee, but not come nigh thee"—seem to be entirely contradicted by experience which testifies that "there is one event to the evil and the good," and that, in epidemics or other widespread disasters, we all, the good and the bad, God-fearers and God-blasphemers, do fare alike, and that the conditions of exemption from physical evil are physical and not spiritual. It is of no use trying to persuade ourselves that that is not so. We shall understand God's dealings with us, and get to the very throbbing heart of such promises as these in this psalm far better, if we start from the certainty that whatever it means it does *not* mean that, with regard to external calamities and disasters, we are going to be God's petted children, or to be saved from the things that fall upon other people. No! no! we have to go a great deal deeper than that. If we have felt a difficulty, as I suppose we all have sometimes, and are ready to say with the half-despondent psalmist, "My feet were almost gone; my steps had well nigh slipped"; when we see what we think the complicated mysteries of the Divine providence in this world, we have to come to the belief that the evil that is in the evil will never come near a man sheltered beneath God's wing. The physical external event may be entirely the same to him as to another who is not covered with His feathers. Here are two partners in a business, the one a Christian man, and the other not. A common disaster overwhelms them. They become bankrupts. Is insolvency the same to the one as it is to the other? Here are two men on board a ship, the one putting his trust in God, the other thinking it all nonsense to trust anything but himself. They are both drowned. Is drowning the same to the two? As their corpses lie side by side among the ooze, with the weeds over them, and the lobsters at them, you may say of the one, but only of the one, "There shall no evil befall thee, neither shall any plague come nigh thy dwelling."

For the protection that is granted to faith is only to be understood by faith. It is deliverance from the evil in the evil which vindicates as no exaggeration, nor as merely an experience and a promise peculiar to the old theocracy of Israel, but not now realized—the grand sayings of this text. The poison is all wiped off the arrow by that Divine protection. It may still wound, but it does not putrefy the flesh. The sewage water comes down, but it passes into the filtering bed, and is disinfected and cleansed before it is permitted to flow over our fields.

And so, brethren, if any of you are finding that the psalm is not outwardly true, and that through the covering wing the storm of hail has come and beaten you down, do not suppose that that in the slightest degree impinges upon the reality and truthfulness of this great promise, "He shall cover thee with his feathers." Anything that has come through *them* is manifestly not an "evil." "Who is he that will harm you, if ye be followers of that which is good?" "If God be for us, who can be against us?" Not what the world calls, and our wrung hearts feel that it rightly calls, "sorrows" and "afflictions"—these all work for our good; and protection consists, not in averting the blows, but in changing their character.

Then, there is another region far higher, in which this promise of my text is absolutely true—that is, in the region of spiritual defense. For no man that lies under the shadow of God, and has his heart filled with the continual consciousness of that presence, is likely to fall before the assaults of evil that tempt him away from God; and the defense which He gives in that region is yet more magnificently impregnable than the defense which He gives against external evils. For, as the New Testament teaches us, we are kept from sin, not by any outward breastplate or armor, nor even by the Divine wing lying above us to cover us, but by the indwelling Christ in our hearts. His Spirit within us makes us free from the law of sin and death, and conquerors over all temptations.

I say not a word about all the other beautiful and pathetic associations which are connected with this emblem of the covering wing, sweet and inexhaustible as it is, but I simply leave with you the two thoughts that I have dwelt upon, of the twofold manner of that Divine protection.

II. And now a word, in the second place, about the flight of the shelterless to the Shelter.

The word which is rendered in our Authorized Version, "shalt thou trust," is, like all Hebrew words for mental and spiritual emotions and actions, strongly metaphorical. It might have been better to retain its literal meaning here instead of substituting the abstract word "trust." That is to say, it would have been an improvement, if we had read with the Revised Version, not, "under his wings shalt thou trust," but "under his wings shalt thou take refuge." For that is the idea which is really conveyed; and in many of the psalms, if you will remember, the same metaphor is employed. "Hide me beneath the shadow of thy wings"; "Beneath thy wings will I take refuge, until calamities are overpast"; and the like. Many such passages will, no doubt, occur to your memories.

But what I wish to signalize is just this, that in this emblem of flying into a refuge from impending perils we get a far more vivid conception, and a far more useful one, as it seems to me, of what Christian faith really is than we derive from many learned volumes and much theological hairsplitting. "Under his wings shalt thou flee for refuge"—is not that a vivid, intense, picturesque, but most illuminative way of telling us what is the very essence, and what is the urgency, and what is the worth, of what we call faith? The Old Testament is full of the teaching—which is masked to ordinary readers, but is the same teaching as the New Testament is confessedly full of—of the necessity of faith as the one bond that binds men to God. If only our translators had wisely determined upon a uniform rendering in Old and New Testament of words that are synonymous, the reader would have seen what is often now reserved for the student, that all these sayings in the Old Testament about "trusting in God" run on all fours with "believe on the Lord Jesus Christ and thou shalt be saved."

But just mark what comes out of that metaphor; that "trust," the faith which unites with God, and brings a man beneath the shadow of His wings, is nothing more nor less than the flying into the refuge that is provided for us. Does that not speak to us of the urgency of the case? Does that not speak to us eloquently of the perils which environ us? Does it not speak to us of the necessity of flight, swift, with all the powers of our will? Is the faith which is a flying into a refuge fairly described as an intellectual act of believing in a testimony? Surely it is something a great deal more than that. A man out in the plain, with the avenger of blood, hot-breathed and bloody-minded, behind him might believe, as much as he liked, that there would be safety within the walls of the City of Refuge, but unless he took to his heels without loss of time, the spear would be in his back before he knew where he was. There are plenty of men that know all about the security of the Refuge, and believe it utterly, but never run for it, and so never get into it. Faith is the gathering up of the whole powers of the nature to fling myself into the asylum, to cast myself into God's arms, to take shelter beneath the shadow of His wings. And unless a man does that, and swiftly, he is exposed to every bird of prey in the sky, and to every beast of prey lurking in wait for him.

The metaphor tells us, too, what are the limits and the worth of faith. A man is not saved because he believes that he is saved, but because by believing he lays hold of the salvation. It is not the flight that is impregnable, and makes those behind its strong bulwarks secure. Not my outstretched hand, but a Hand that my hand grasps, is what holds me up. The power of faith is but that it brings me into contact with God, and sets me behind the sevenfold bastions of the Almighty protection.

So, brethren, another consideration comes out of this clause: "Under his wings shalt thou trust." If you do not flee for refuge to that wing, it is of no use to you, however expanded it is, however soft and downy its underside, however sure its protection. You remember the passage where our Lord uses the same venerable figure with modifications, and says: "How often would I have gathered thy children together, as a hen doth gather her brood under her wings, *and ye would not.*" So our "would not" thwarts Christ's "would." Flight to the refuge is the condition of being saved. How can a man get shelter by any other way than by running to the shelter? The wing is expanded; it is for us to say whether we will flee "for refuge to the hope set before us."

III. Now, lastly, the warrant for this flight.

"His truth shall be thy shield." Now, "truth" here does not mean the body of revealed words, which are often called God's truth, but it describes a certain characteristic of the Divine nature. And if, instead of "truth," we read the good old English word "troth" we should be a great deal nearer understanding what the psalmist meant. Or if "troth" is archaic, and conveys little meaning to us; suppose we substitute a somewhat longer word, of the same meaning, and say, "His faithfulness shall be thy shield." You cannot trust a God that has not given you an inkling of his character or disposition, but if he has spoken, then you "know where to have him." That is just what the psalmist means. How can a man be encouraged to fly into a refuge, unless he is absolutely sure that there is an entrance for him into it, and that, entering, he is safe? And that security is provided in the great thought of God's troth. "Thy faithfulness is like the great mountains." "Who is like unto thee, O Lord; or to thy faithfulness round about thee?" That faithfulness shall be our "shield," not a tiny targe that a man could bear upon his left arm, but the word means the large shield, planted in the ground in front of the soldier, covering him, however hot the fight, and circling him around, like a tower of iron.

God is "faithful" to all the obligations under which He has come by making us. That is what one of the New Testament writers tells us, when he speaks about Him as "a faithful Creator." Then, if He has put desires into our hearts, be sure that somewhere there is their satisfaction; and if He has given us needs, be sure that in Him there is the supply; and if He has lodged in us aspirations which make us restless, be sure that if we will turn them to Him, they will be satisfied and we shall be at rest. "God never sends mouths but He sends meat to fill them." "He remembers our frame," and measures His dealings accordingly. When He made me, He bound Himself to make it possible that I should be blessed for ever; and He has done it.

God is faithful to His word, according to that great saying in the epistle to the Hebrews, where the writer tells us that by "God's counsel," and "God's oath," "two immutable things," we might have "strong consolation, who have fled for refuge to lay hold upon the hope set before us."

God is faithful to His own past. The more He has done the more He will do. "Thou hast been my help; leave me not, neither forsake me." Therein we present a plea which God Himself will honor. And He is faithful to His own past in a yet wider sense. For all the revelations of His love and of His grace in times that are gone, though they might be miraculous in their form, are permanent in their essence. So one of the psalmists, hundreds of years after the time that Israel was led through the wilderness, sang: "There did we"—of this present generation—"rejoice in Him." What has been, is, and will be, for Thou art "the same yesterday, and today, and forever."

We have no God that lurks in darkness, but One that has come into the light. We have to run, not into a refuge that is built upon a "perhaps," but upon "Verily, verily, I say unto thee." Let us build rock upon rock, and let our faith correspond to the faithfulness of Him that has promised.

O Lord, our gracious Father! we would rejoice in Thee, and bless Thee for all the peace and pure, lasting gladness which flow into hearts that are at rest in God. Thou knowest how often we have sought to hew out for ourselves cisterns, and they have proved to be broken, that could hold no water.

But we beseech Thee that Thou wouldst help us, made wise by experience, if so it be that our experiences have taught us, and made wise by Thy Spirit at all events, to withdraw our hearts from earth and to set them steadfastly upon God. May we all seek first the Kingdom and the righteousness. May we all live for something higher and nobler than self and self-pleasing. May we not only feel the presence of duty but the impulse of love. And may we serve Thee with glad hearts, and bring to Thee the acceptable offering of grateful and devout spirits.

O Lord! we praise Thee for the great things and the small things, for the gifts that perish with the using, and for the gifts that grow by use. For all the past, its sorrows and its losses as well as its gifts and its joys; for all the present, its duties and difficulties as well as delights, and for all that future of unmingled and manifest and ineffable good, we desire to praise Thee, and beseech Thee that Thou wouldst grant us Thy gracious help and presence in our worship this evening; for the sake of Jesus Christ our Saviour Lord. Amen.[2]

---

[2] From *Pulpit Prayers*.

THE FIRE OF GOD [1]

To "*dwell with everlasting burnings*" means two things. First, it means to hold a familiar intercourse and communion with God. The question which presents itself to thoughtful minds is, What sort of a man must I be if I am to dwell near God? The lowliest bush may be lit by the Divine fire, and not be consumed by it; and the poorest heart may be all aflame with an indwelling God, if only it yield itself to Him, and long for His likeness. Electricity only flames into consuming fire when its swift passage is resisted. The question for us all is, how can I receive this Holy fire into my bosom, and not be burned? Is any communion possible, and if it be, on what conditions? It is the question which the heart of man is really asking, though it knows not the meaning of its own unrest.

---

[1] From *Similes and Figures from Alexander Maclaren*, by Francis E. Clark. Copyright, 1910, by Fleming H. Revell, and reprinted by permission.

11. THE CHRISTIAN ATTITUDE TO SOCIAL SINS [1]

───────────────

"And have no fellowship with the unfruitful works of darkness, but rather reprove them." EPH. 5:11.

We have seen in a former sermon that "the fruit," or outcome, "of the Light" is a comprehensive perfection, consisting in all sorts and degrees of goodness and righteousness and truth. Therefore, the commandment, "Walk as children of light," sums up all Christian morality. Is there need, then, for any additional precept? Yes; for Christian people do not live in an empty world. If there were no evil round them, and no proclivity to evil within them, it would be amply sufficient to say to them, "Be true to the light which you behold." But since both these things are, the commandment of my text is further necessary. We do not work in *vacuo,* and therefore friction and atmosphere have to be taken account of; and an essential part of "walking as children of the light" is to know how to behave ourselves when confronted with "the works of darkness."

These Ephesian Christians lived in a state of society honeycombed with hideous immorality, the center of which was the temple, which was their city's glory and shame. It was all but impossible for them to have nothing to do with the works of evil, unless, indeed, they went out of the world. But the difficulty of obedience does not affect the duty of obedience, nor slacken in the smallest degree the stringency of a command. This obligation lies upon us as fully as it did upon them, and the discharge of it by professing Christians would bring new life to moribund churches.

I. Let me ask you to note with me, first, the fruitlessness inherent in all the works of darkness.

You may remember that I pointed out, in a former discourse, on

---
[1] From *Christ's Musts,* Hodder & Stoughton Ltd. (London). Reprinted by permission.

the context, that the Apostle, here and elsewhere, draws a very significant distinction between "works" and "fruit," and that distinction is put very strikingly in the words of my text. There are works which are barren. It is a grim thought that there may be abundant activity which, in the eyes of God, comes to just nothing; and that pages and pages of laborious calculations, when all summed up, have for result a great round O. Men are busy, and hosts of them are doing what the old fairy stories tell us that evil spirits were condemned to do—spinning ropes out of sea sand; and their lifework is naught when you come to reckon it up.

I have no time to dwell upon this thought, but I wish, just for a moment or two, to illustrate it.

All godless life is fruitless, inasmuch as it has no permanent results. Permanent results of a sort, indeed, follow everything that men do, for all our actions tend to make character, and they all have a share in fixing that which depends upon character—viz., destiny, both here and yonder. And thus the most fleeting of our deeds, which in one aspect is as transitory as the snow upon the great plains when the sun rises, leaves everlasting traces upon ourselves and upon our condition. But yet acts concerned with transitory things may have permanent fruit, or may be as transient as the things with which they are concerned. And the difference depends on the spirit in which they are done. If the roots are only in the surface skin of soil, when that is pared off the plant goes. A life that is to be eternal must strike its roots through all the superficial *humus* down to the very heart of things. When its roots twine themselves round God, then the deeds which blossom from them will blossom unfading for ever.

Think of men going empty-handed into another world, and saying, "O Lord! I made a big fortune in Manchester when I lived there, and I left it all behind me"; or, "I mastered a science, and one gleam of the light of eternity has antiquated it"; or, "I gained prizes, won my aims, and they have all dropped from my hands, and here I stand, having to say in the most tragic sense: Nothing in my hands I bring." And another man dies in the Lord, and his "works do follow" him. It is not every vintage that bears exportation. Some wines are mellowed by crossing the ocean; some are turned into vinegar. The works of darkness are unfruitful because they are transient.

And they are unfruitful because, whilst they last they yield no real satisfaction. The Apostle could say to another Church with a certainty as to what the answer would be, "What fruit had ye *then*"—when ye were doing them—"in the things whereof ye are now ashamed?" And the answer is "None!" Of course, it is true that men do bad things because they like them better than good. Of course, it is true that the misery of mankind is that they have no appetite in the general for the only real satisfaction. But it is also true that no man who feeds his heart and mind on anything short of God is really at rest in anything that he does or possesses. Occasional twinges of conscience, dim perceptions that after all they are walking in a vain show, glimpses of nobler possibilities, a vague unrest, an unwillingness to reflect and look the facts of their condition in the face, like men that will not take stock because they half suspect that they are insolvent—these are the conditions that attach to all godless men's lives. There is no real fruit for their thirsty lips to feed upon. The smallest man is too large to be satisfied with anything short of Infinity. The human heart is like some narrow opening on a hillside, so narrow that it looks as if a glassful of water would fill it. But it goes away down, down, down into the depths of the mountain, and you may pour in hogsheads and no effect is visible. God, and God alone, brings to the thirsty heart the fruit that it needs.

Another solemn thought illustrates the unfruitfulness of a godless life. There is no correspondence between what such a man does and what he is intended to do. Think of what the most degraded and sensuous wretch that shambles about the slums of a city, sodden with beer and rotten with profligacy, could be. Think of the raptures of devout contemplation and the energies of holy work which are possible for that soul, and then say—though it is an extreme case, the principle holds in less extreme cases—"Are these things that men do apart from God, however shining, noble, illustrious they may be in the eyes of the world, and trumpeted forth by the mouthpieces of popular opinion, are these things worth calling fruits fit to be borne by such a tree?" No more than the cankers on a rosebush or the galls on an oak tree are worthy of being called fruit are these works that some of you have as the only products of a life's activity. "Wherefore, when I looked that it should bring forth grapes, brought it forth wild grapes."

II. And now, secondly, notice the plain Christian duty of abstinence. "Have no fellowship with the unfruitful works of darkness." Now, the text, as it stands in our version, seems to suggest that these dark works are personified as companions whom a good man ought to avoid; and that, therefore, the bearing of the exhortation is "Have nothing to do, in your own individual lives, with evil things that one man can commit." But I take it that, important as that injunction and prohibition is, the Apostle's meaning is somewhat different, and that my text would perhaps be more accurately translated if another word were substituted for "have no fellowship with." The original expression seems rather to mean, "Do not go partners with other people in works of darkness, which it takes more than one to commit." Or, to put it into other language, the Apostle is regarding Christian people here as members of society, and exhorting them to a certain course of conduct in reference to plain and palpable existing evils around them. And such an exhortation to the duty of plain abstinence from things that the opinion of the world around us has no objection to, but which are contrary to the light, is addressed to all Christian people.

The need of it I do not require to illustrate at any length. But let me remind you that the devil has no more cunning way of securing a long lease of life for any evil than getting Christian people and Christian churches to give it their sanction. What was it that kept slavery alive for centuries? Largely, that Christian men solemnly declared that it was a Divine institution. What is it that has kept war alive for all these centuries? Largely, that bishops and preachers have always been ready to bless colors, and to read a christening service over a man-of-war—and, I suppose, to ask God that an eighty-ton gun might be blessed to smash our enemies to pieces, and not to blow our sailors to bits. And what is it that preserves the crying evils of our community, the immoralities, the drunkenness, the trade dishonesty, and all the other things that I do not need to remind you of in the pulpit? Largely this, that professing Christians are mixed up with them. If only the whole body of those who profess and call themselves Christians would shake their hands clear of all complicity with such things, they could not last. Individual responsibility for collective action needs to be far more solemnly laid to heart by professing Christians than ever it has been.

Nor need I remind you, I suppose, with what fatal effects on the Gospel and the Church itself all such complicity is attended. Even the companions of wrongdoers despise, whilst they fraternize with, the professing Christian who has no higher standard than their own. What was it that made the Church victorious over the combined forces of imperial persecution, pagan superstition, and philosophic speculation? I believe that among all the causes that a well-known historian has laid down for the triumph of Christianity what was as powerful as—I was going to say even more than—the gospel of peace and love which the Church proclaimed was the standard of austere morality which it held up to a world rotting in its own filth. And sure I am that wherever the Church says, "So do I, because of the fear of the Lord," it will gain a power, and will be regarded with a possibly reluctant, but a very real, respect which no easygoing coming down to the level of popular moralities will ever secure for a silver-slippered Christianity. And so, brethren, I would say to you, Do not be afraid of the old name *Puritan*. Ignorant people use it as a scoff. It should be a crown of glory. "Have no fellowship with the unfruitful works of darkness."

But how is this to be done? Well, of course, there is only one way of abstaining, and that is, to abstain. But there are a great many different ways of abstaining. Light is not fire. And the more that Christian people feel themselves bound to stand aloof from common evils, the more are they bound to see that they do it in the spirit of the Master, which is meekness. It is always an invidious position to take up. And if we take it up with any heat and temper, with any lack of moderation, with any look of ostentation of superior righteousness, or with any trace of the Boanerges spirit which says, "Let us call down fire from heaven and consume them," our testimony will be weakened, and the world will have a right to say to us, "Jesus we know, and Paul we know; but who are ye?" "Who made this man a judge and a divider over us?" "In meekness instructing them that oppose themselves."

III. Lastly, note the still harder Christian duty of vigorous protest.

The further duty beyond abstinence which the text enjoins is inadequately represented by our version, "but rather reprove them." For the word rendered in our version "reprove" is the same which our Lord employed when He spoke of the mission of the Comforter as being to "convince [or convict] the world of sin." And it does not merely mean "reprove," but so to reprove as to produce the conviction which is the object of the reproof.

This task is laid on the shoulders of all professing Christians. A *silent* abstinence is not enough. No doubt, the best way, in some circumstances, to convict the darkness is to shine. Our holiness will convict sin of its ugliness. Our light will reveal the gloom. The presentation of a Christian life is the Christian man's mightiest weapon in his conflict with the world's evil. But that is not all. And if Christian people think that they have done all their duty, in regard of clamant and common iniquities, by simply abstaining from them and presenting a nobler example, they have yet to learn one very important chapter of their duty. A dumb church is a dying church, and it ought to be. For Christ has sent us here in order, amongst other things, that we may bring Christian principles to bear upon the actions of the community, and not be afraid to speak when we are called upon by conscience to do so.

Now I am not going to dwell upon this matter, but I want to point out to you how, in the context here, there are two or three very important principles glanced at which bear upon it. And one of them is this, that one reason for speaking out is the very fact that the evils are so evil that a man is ashamed to speak about them. Did you ever notice this context, in which the Apostle, in the next verse to my text, gives the reason for his commandment to "reprove" thus: *"For* it is a shame even to speak of those things which are done of them in secret"? Did you ever hear of a fantastic tenderness for morality so very sensitive that it is not at all shocked when the immoral things are *done,* but glows with virtuous indignation when a Christian man speaks out about them? There are plenty of people nowadays who tell us that it is "indelicate" and "indecent" and "improper," and I do not know how much else, for a Christian teacher or minister to say a word about certain moral scandals. But they do not say anything about the immorality and the indelicacy and the indecency of doing them. Let us have done with that hypocrisy, brethren. I am arguing for no disregard for proprieties; I want all fitting reticence observed, and I do not wish indiscriminate rebukes to be flung at foul things; but it is too much to require that, by reason of the very inky cloud of filth that they fling up like cuttlefish, they should escape censure. Let us remember Paul's exhortation, and reprove *because* the things are too bad to be spoken about.

Further, note in the context the thought that the conviction of the darkness comes from the flashing upon it of the light. "All things when they are reproved are made manifest by the light." Which, being translated into other words, is this: Be strong in your brave protest, because it only needs that the thing should be seen as it is, and called by its right name, in order to be condemned.

The Assyrians had a belief that if ever by any chance a demon saw himself in a mirror, he was frightened at his own ugliness and incontinently fled. And if Christian people would only hold up the mirror of Christian principle to the hosts of evil things that afflict our city and our country, they would vanish like ghosts at sunrise. They cannot stand the light; therefore let us cast the light upon them.

And do not forget the other final principle here, which is imperfectly represented by our translation. We ought to read, "Whatever is made manifest is light." Yes. In the physical world when light falls upon a thing you see it, because there is on it a surface of light. And in the moral world the intention of all this conviction is that the thing disclosed to be darkness should, in the very disclosure, cease to be dark, should forsake its nature and be transformed into light. Such transformation is not always the case. Alas! there are ebon glooms on which the light falls, and it does nothing. But the purpose in all cases should be, and the issue in many will be, that the merciful conviction by the light will be followed by the conversion of darkness into light.

And so, dear brethren, I bring this text to your hearts, and lay it upon your consciences. We may not all be called upon to speak; we are all called upon to *be*. You can shine, and by shining show how dark the darkness is. The obligation is laid upon us all; the commandment still comes to every Christian which was given to the old prophet, "Declare unto my people their transgression, and to the house of Jacob their sins." A quaint old writer says that the presence of a saint "hinders the devil's elbow-room to do his tricks." We can all rebuke sin by our righteousness, and by our shining reveal the darkness to itself. We do not walk as children of the light unless we keep ourselves from all connivance with works of darkness, and by all means at our disposal reprove and convict them. "Come out from among them, and be ye separate . . . and touch no unclean thing, saith the Lord."

O Lord! our God and Father, Who art always near us, and ready to hear our lowest supplication, and to answer our feeblest desire, we would come to Thee this morning needy and weak, and cast ourselves on Thy great promises, and on the faithful love which has fulfilled these in the past.

We beseech Thee to help us to draw near to Thee now, and in the depths of our hearts may we turn to Thee and cling to Thee, and desire from Thee the greatest of gifts, the gift of Thy Divine Spirit, to dwell in us. O Lord! we thank Thee that with all our weakness and deadness and sin Thou dost yet not disdain to enter into our hearts, and in their narrow and stained space to manifest Thy greatness, Thy transforming power, and Thy peace-bringing love. We beseech Thee that each of us, whatever may be the variety of our conditions and wants, may feel that we are really in touch with Thee, and that it is no vain thing either to speak to Thee or to listen to Thy voice to us.

We beseech Thee to hallow our hearts; to draw near in the fullness of Thy grace; to forgive all that has been wrong in the past; and to establish, strengthen and settle us, in good and in union with Thyself; through Jesus Christ our Lord and Saviour. Amen.[2]

---

[2] From *Pulpit Prayers*.

CHURCHES THAT HELP [1]

Through all life the deliverance goes on, the deliverance from sin, the deliverance from wrath. The Christian salvation, then, is a process begun at conversion, carried on progressively through life, and reaching its climax in another state. Day by day, through the spring and the early summer, the sun is longer in the sky, and rises higher in the heavens. And the path of the Christian is as the shining light. Last year's greenwood is this year's hardwood; and the Christian, in like manner, has to grow in the grace and knowledge of the Lord and Saviour. So these progressively, and, therefore, as yet imperfectly saved people, are gathered into the Church.

If that be the description of the kind of folk that come into a Christian church, the duties of that church are very plainly marked. There are Christian churches into which, if a young plant is brought it is pretty sure to be killed. The temperature is so low that the tender shoots are burned as with frost, and die. Let us, dear friends, remember that a Christian church is a nursery of imperfect Christians, and, for ourselves and for one another, try to make our communion such as shall help shy and tender graces to unfold themselves, and woo out by the encouragement of example the lowest and the least perfect to lofty holiness and consecration like the Master's.

---

[1] From *Similes and Figures from Alexander Maclaren,* by Francis E. Clark. Copyright, 1910, by Fleming H. Revell, and reprinted by permission.

12. MAHANAIM: THE TWO CAMPS [1]

"And Jacob went on his way, and the angels of God met him. And when Jacob saw them, he said, This is God's host: and he called the name of that place Mahanaim (i.e., two camps)." GEN. 32:1, 2.

This vision came at a crisis in Jacob's life. He has just left the house of Laban, his father-in-law, where he had lived for many years, and in company with a long caravan, consisting of wives, children, servants, and all his wealth turned into cattle, is journeying back again to Palestine. His road leads him close by the country of Esau. Jacob was no soldier, and he is naturally terrified to meet his justly incensed brother. And so, as he plods along with his defenseless company trailing behind him, and as you may see the Arab caravans streaming over the same uplands today, all at once, in the middle of his march, a bright-harnessed army of angels meets him. Whether visible to the eye of sense, or, as would appear, only to the eye of faith, they *are* visible to this troubled man; and, in a glow of confident joy, he calls the name of that place "Mahanaim," two camps. One camp was the little one of his down here, with the helpless women and children and his own frightened and defenseless self, and the other was the great one up there, or rather in shadowy but most real spiritual presence around about him, as a bodyguard making an impregnable wall between him and every foe. We may take some very plain and everlastingly true lessons out of this story.

I. First, the angels of God meet us on the dusty road of common life. "Jacob went on his way, and the angels of God met him."

As he was tramping along there, over the lonely fields of Edom, with many a thought on his mind and many a fear at his heart, but feeling, "There is the path that I have to walk on," all at once the air was filled with the soft rustle of angel wings, and the brightness from the flashing

---
[1] From *Christ in the Heart*, Hodder & Stoughton Ltd. (London). Reprinted by permission.

armor of the heavenly hosts flamed across his unexpecting eye. And so is it evermore. The true place for us to receive visions of God is in the path of the homely, prosaic duties which He lays upon us. The dusty road is far more likely to be trodden by angel feet than the remote summits of the mountain, where we sometimes would fain go; and many an hour consecrated to devotion has less of the manifest presence of God than is granted to some weary heart in its commonplace struggle with the little troubles and trials of daily life. These make the doors, as it were, by which the visitants draw near to us.

It is the common duties, "The narrow round, the daily task," that not only give us "all we ought to ask," but are the selected means and channels by which, ever, God's visitants draw near to us. The man that has never seen an angel standing beside him, and driving his loom for him, or helping him at his counter and his desk, and the woman that has never seen an angel, according to the bold realism and homely vision of the old German picture, working with her in the kitchen and preparing the meal for the household, have little chance of meeting such visitants at any other point of their experience or event of their lives.

If the week be empty of the angels, you will never catch sight of a feather of their wings on the Sunday. And if we do not recognize their presence in the midst of all the prose, and the commonplace, and the vulgarity, and the triviality, and the monotony, the dust of the small duties, we shall go up to the summit of Sinai itself and see nothing there but cold gray stone and everlasting snows. "Jacob went on his way, and the angels of God met him." The true field for religion is the field of common life.

And then another side of the same thought is this, that it is in the path where God has bade us walk that we shall find the angels round us. We may meet them, indeed, on paths of our own choosing, but it will be the sort of angel that Balaam met, with a sword in his hand, mighty and beautiful, but wrathful too; and we had better not front him! But the friendly helpers, the emissaries of God's love, the Apostles of His grace, do not haunt the roads that we make for ourselves. They confine themselves rigidly to "the paths in which God has before ordained that we should walk in them." A man has no right to expect, and he will not get blessing and help and Divine gifts when, self-willedly, he has taken the bit between his teeth, and is choosing his own road in the world. But if he will say, "Lord! here I am; put me where Thou wilt, and do with me what Thou wilt," then he may be sure that that path, though it may be solitary of human companionship, and leading up amongst barren rocks and over bare moorlands, where the sun beats down fiercely, will not be unvisited by a better presence, so that in sweet consciousness of sufficiency of rich grace, he shall be able to say, "I, being in the way, the Lord led me."

II. Still further, we may draw from this incident the lesson that God's angels meet us punctually at the hour of need.

Jacob is drawing nearer and nearer to his fear every step. He is now just on the borders of Esau's country, and close upon opening communications with his brother. At that critical moment, just before the finger of the clock has reached the point on the dial at which the bell would strike, the needed help comes, the angel guards draw near and camp beside him. It is always so. "The Lord shall help her, and that right early." His hosts come no sooner and no later than we need. If they appeared before we had realized our danger and our defenselessness, our hearts would not leap up at their coming, as men in a beleaguered town do when the guns of the relieving force are heard booming from afar. Often God's delays seem to us inexplicable, and our prayers to have no more effect than if they were spoken to a sleeping Baal. But such delays are merciful. They help us to the consciousness of our need. They let us feel the presence of the sorrow. They give opportunity of proving the weakness of all other supports. They test and increase desire for His help. They throw us more unreservedly into His arms. They afford room for the sorrow or the burden to work its peaceable fruits. So, and in many other ways, delay of succor fits us to receive succor, and our God makes no tarrying but for our sakes.

It is His way to let us come almost to the edge of the precipice, and then, in the very nick of time, when another minute and we are over, to stretch out His strong right hand and save us. So Peter is left in prison, though prayer is going up unceasingly for him—and no answer comes. The days of the Passover feast slip away, and still he is in prison, and prayer does nothing for him. The last day of his life, according to Herod's purpose, dawns, and all the day the Church lifts up its voice—but apparently there is no answer, nor any that regarded. The night comes, and still the vain cry goes up, and Heaven seems deaf or apathetic. The night wears on, and still no help comes. But in the last watch of that last night, when day is almost dawning, at nearly the last minute when escape would have been possible, the angel touches the sleeping Apostle, and with leisurely calmness, as sure that he had ample time, leads him out to freedom and safety. It was precisely because Jesus loved the household at Bethany that, after receiving the sister's message, He abode still for two days in the same place where He was. However our impatience may wonder and our faithlessness venture sometimes almost to rebuke Him when He comes with words like Mary's and Martha's—"Lord, if Thou hadst been here, such and such sorrows would not have happened, and Thou couldst so easily have been here"—we should learn the lesson that even if He has delayed so long that the dreaded blow has fallen, He has come soon enough to make it the occasion for a still more glorious communication of His power.

Rest in the Lord, wait patiently for Him, and He shall give thee the desires of thine heart.

III. Again, we learn from this incident that the angels of God come in the shape which we need.

Jacob's want at the moment was protection. Therefore the angels appear in warlike guise, and present before the defenseless man another camp, in which he and his unwieldy caravan of women and children and cattle may find security. If his special want had been of some blessing of another kind, no doubt another form of appearance suited with precision to his need would have been imposed upon these angel helpers. For God's gifts to us change their character, as the Rabbis fabled that the manna tasted to each man what each most desired. The same pure Heavenly bread has the varying savor that commends it to varying palates. God's grace is Protean. It takes all the forms that man's necessities require. As water assumes the shape of any vessel into which it is put, so this great blessing comes to each of us, molded according to the pressure and taking the form of our circumstances and necessities. His fullness is all-sufficient. It is the same blood that, passing to all the members, ministers to each according to the needs and fashion of each. And it is the same grace which, passing to our souls, in each man is shaped according to his present condition and ministers to his present wants.

So, dear brethren, in that great fullness each of us may have the thing that we need. The angel who to one man is protection, to another shall be teaching and inspiration; to another shall appear with chariots of fire and horses of fire to sweep the rapt soul heavenward; to another shall draw near as a deliverer from his fetters, at whose touch the bonds shall fall from off him; to another shall appear as the instructor in duty and the appointer of a path of service, like that vision that shone in the castle to the Apostle Paul, and said, "Thou must bear witness for me at Rome"; to another shall appear as opening the door of Heaven and letting a flood of light come down upon his darkened heart, as to the apocalyptic seer in his rocky Patmos. And all this worketh that one and the selfsame Lord of angels dividing to every man severally as He will, and as the man needs. The defenseless Jacob has the manifestation of the Divine presence in the guise of armed warriors that guard his unwarlike camp.

I add one last word. Long centuries after Jacob's experience at Mahanaim, another trembling fugitive found himself there, fearful, like Jacob, of the vengeance and anger of one who was knit to him by blood. When poor King David was flying from the face of Absalom his son, the first place where he made a stand, and where he remained during the whole of the rebellion, was this town of Mahanaim, away on the eastern side of the Jordan. Do you not think that to the kingly exile, in his feebleness and his fear, the very name of his resting place would be an omen? Would he not recall the old story, and bethink himself of how round that other frightened man "Bright-harnessed angels stood in order serviceable"; and would he not, as he looked on his little band of friends, faithful among the faithless, have his eyesight cleared to behold the other camp? Such a vision, no doubt, inspired the calm confidence of the psalm which evidently belongs to that dark hour of his life, and made it possible for the hunted king, with his feeble band, to sing even then, "I will both lay me down in peace, and sleep: for Thou, Lord, makest me dwell in safety, solitary though I am."

Nor is the vision emptied of its power to stay and make brave by all the ages that have passed. The vision was for a moment; the fact is forever. The sun's ray was flashed back from celestial armor; "the next all unreflected shone" on the lonely wastes of the desert—but the host of God was there still. The transitory appearance of the permanent realities is a revelation to us as truly as to the patriarch; and though no angel wings may winnow the air around our road, nor any sworded seraphim be seen on our commonplace march, we too have all the armies of Heaven with us, if we tread the path which God has marked out, and in our weakness and trembling commit ourselves to Him. The heavenly warriors die not, and hover around us today, excelling in the strength of their immortal youth, and as ready to succor us as they were all these centuries ago to guard the solitary Jacob.

Better still, the "Captain of the Lord's host" is "come up" to be our defense, and our faith has not only to behold the many ministering spirits sent forth to minister to us, but One mightier than they, Whose commands they all obey, and Who Himself is the companion of our solitude and the shield of our defenselessness. It was blessed that Jacob should be met by the many angels of God. It is infinitely more blessed that "*the* angel of the Lord"—the One who is more than the many—"encampeth round about them that fear Him, and delivereth them."

The postscript of the last letter which Gordon sent from Khartoum closed with the words, "The hosts are with me—Mahanaim." Were they not, even though death was near? Was that sublime faith a mistake—the vision an optical delusion? No, for their ranks are arrayed around God's children to keep them from all evil while He wills that they should love, and their chariots of fire and horses of fire are sent to bear them to Heaven when He wills that they should die.

O Lord! look upon us this morning, desiring, we trust, to seek Thy face, and bringing ourselves to Thee with thankful surrender, and longing that we may possess Thee more and more, and be more possessed by Thee. We bless Thee for every benefit received at Thy hand. The eyes of all things wait on Thee, and Thou givest them their meat in due season. Thou givest us the better food which Thou hast made us to long for.

But we praise Thee, too, for the lesser gifts of Thy hands, and extol that gracious Name Whose tender mercies are over all His works. We would bow before the majesty of Thy greatness. We would draw near, attracted by the greatness of Thy mercy and compassion. We would bow ourselves with submissive wills as the subjects of that Kingdom which is an everlasting dominion. We pray that the things seen and temporal, by which Thou dost often introduce the great message of Thy love to us, may be precious to us, not only for their own sakes nor by reason of the passing delight and satisfaction which they may bring, but because they help us to apprehend more fully the Unseen and Eternal love of the Infinite heart of God.

O Lord! be near each of us as we may severally require. Speak in our hearts, and, if it please Thee, speak through our lips, and let Thy word be to each of us what Thou dost mean it to be, the medium of Eternal life. We pray Thee to hear and to accept us, for our Lord Christ's sake. Amen.[2]

---

[2] From *Pulpit Prayers*.

MAKING OUR OWN CLOTHING [1]

The great law of community and increase, so that the dispositions cultivated here rise to sovereign power hereafter, and what was tendency and struggle and imperfect realization upon earth becomes fact and complete possession in the heavens gives solemn importance to the smallest of our victories or defeats here on earth! They are threads in the web out of which our garment is to be cut. After all, yonder as here, we are dressed in homespun, and we make our clothing and shape it for our wear.

That truth is perfectly consistent with the other truth on which it reposes, that the Christian man owes to Christ the reception of the new garment of purity and holiness. The evangelical doctrine, "not by works of righteousness which we have done," and its complement in the words of my text are perfectly harmonious. We cannot weave the web except Christ gives us the yarn, nor can we work out our own salvation except Christ bestows upon us the salvation which we work out. The two things go together. Let us remember that, whilst in one aspect the souls that were all clad in filthy garments are arrayed as a bridegroom decketh his bride with a fair vesture, in another aspect we ourselves, by our own efforts, by our own struggles, by our own victories, have to weave, and fashion, and cut, and sew the dress which we shall wear forever.

[1] From *Similes and Figures from Alexander Maclaren*, by Francis E. Clark. Copyright, 1910, by Fleming H. Revell, and reprinted by permission.

13. THE WARRIOR PEACE [1]

"The peace of God, which passeth all understanding, shall keep your hearts and minds through Christ Jesus." PHIL. 4:7.

The great Mosque of Constantinople was once a Christian church, dedicated to the Holy Wisdom. Over its western portal may still be read, graven on a brazen plate, the words, "Come unto me, all ye that labor and are heavy laden, and I will give you rest." For four hundred years noisy crowds have fought, and sorrowed, and fretted beneath the dim inscription in an unknown tongue; and no eye has looked at it, nor any heart responded. It is but too sad a symbol of the reception which Christ's offers meet amongst men, and—blessed be His name!—its prominence there, though unread and unbelieved, is a symbol of the patient forbearance with which rejected blessings are once and again pressed upon us, and He stretches out His hand though no man regards, and calls though none do hear. My text is Christ's offer of peace. The world offers excitement; Christ promises repose.

I. Mark, then, first, this peace of God. What is it?

What are its elements? Whence does it come? It is of Him, as being its Source, or Origin, or Author, or Giver, but it belongs to Him in a yet deeper sense, for Himself is Peace. And in some humble but yet real fashion our restless and anxious hearts may partake in the Divine tranquillity, and with a calm repose, kindred with that rest from which it is derived, may enter into His rest.

If that be too high a flight, at all events the peace that may be ours was His, in the perfect and unbroken tranquillity of His perfect Manhood. What, then, are its elements? The peace of God must, first of all, be peace with God. Conscious friendship with Him is indispensable to all true tranquillity. Where that is absent there may be the ignoring of the

---
[1] From *The Unchanging Christ,* Alexander & Shepheard (London), 1889.

disturbed relationship; but there will be no peace of heart. The indispensable requisite is "a conscience like a sea at rest." Unless we have made sure work of our relationship with God, and know that He and we are friends, there is no real repose possible for us. In the whirl of excitement we may forget, and for a time turn away from, the realities of our relation to Him, and so get such gladness as is possible to a life not rooted in conscious friendship with Him. But such lives will be like some of those sunny islands in the eastern Pacific, extinct volcanoes, where Nature smiles and all things are prodigal and life is easy and luxuriant; but some day the clouds gather, and the earth shakes, and fire pours forth, and the sea boils, and every living thing dies, and darkness and desolation come. You are living, brother, upon a volcano's side, unless the roots of your being are fixed in a God who is your Friend.

Again, the peace of God is peace within ourselves. The unrest of human life comes largely from our being torn asunder by contending impulses. Conscience pulls this way, passion that. Desire says, "Do this"; reason, judgment, prudence say, "It is at your peril if you do!" One desire fights against another. And so the man is rent asunder. There must be the harmonizing of all the being if there is to be real rest of spirit. No longer must it be like the chaos ere the creative word was spoken, where, in gloom, contending elements strove.

Again, men have not peace, because in most of them everything is topmost that ought to be undermost, and everything undermost that ought to be uppermost. "Beggars are on horseback" (and we know where they ride) "and princes walking." The more regal part of the man's nature is suppressed, and trodden under foot; and the servile arts, which ought to be under firm restraint, and guided by a wise hand, are too often supreme, and wild work comes of that. When you put the captain, and the officers, and everybody on board that knows anything about navigation, into irons, and fasten down the hatches on them, and let the crew and the cabin boys take the helm and direct the ship, it is not likely that the voyage will end anywhere but on the rocks. Multitudes are living lives of unrestfulness, simply because they have set the lowest parts of their nature upon the throne, and subordinated the highest.

Our unrest comes from yet another source. You have not peace, because you have not found and grasped the true objects for any of your faculties. God is the only possession that brings quiet. The heart hungers until it feeds upon Him. The mind is satisfied with no truth until behind truth it finds a Person who is true. The will is enslaved and wretched until in God it recognizes legitimate and absolute authority which it is blessing to obey. Love puts out its yearnings, like the filaments that gossamer spiders send out into the air, seeking in vain for something to fasten upon, until it touches God, and clings there. There is no rest for a man until he rests in God. The reason why this world is so full of excitement is because it is so empty of peace, and the reason why it is so empty of peace is because it is so void of God. The peace of God brings peace with Him, and peace within. It "unites our hearts to fear His name," and draws all the else turbulent and confusedly flowing impulses of the great deep of the spirit after itself, in a tidal wave, as the moon the waters of the gathered ocean. The peace of God is peace with Him, and peace within.

I need not, I suppose, do more than say one word about that descriptive clause in my text, it "passeth understanding." The understanding is not the hand by which men lay hold of the peace of God any more than you can see a picture with your ears or hear music with your eyes. To everything its own organ: you cannot weigh truth in a tradesman's scales or measure thought with a yardstick. Love is not the organ for apprehending Euclid, nor the brain the organ for grasping these Divine and spiritual gifts. The peace of God transcends the understanding, as well as belongs to another order of things than that about which the understanding is concerned. You must experience it to know it; you must have it in order that you may feel its sweetness. It eludes the grasp of the loveliest, though it yields itself to the clutch of the patient and loving heart.

II. So notice, in the next place, what my text tells us about what the peace of God does.

It "shall keep your hearts and minds." The Apostle here blends together, in a very remarkable manner, the conceptions of peace and of war, for he employs a purely military word to express the office of this Divine peace. That word, "shall keep," is the same as is translated in another of his letters "kept with a garrison"—and, though, perhaps, it might be going too far to insist that the military idea is prominent in his mind, it will certainly not be unsafe to recognize its presence.

So, then, this Divine peace takes upon itself warlike functions, and garrisons the heart and mind. What does he mean by "the heart and mind"? Not, as the English reader might suppose, two different faculties, the emotional and the intellectual—which is what we usually roughly mean by our distinction between heart and mind—but, as is always the case in the Bible, the "heart" means the whole inner man, whether considered as thinking, willing, purposing, or doing any other inward act; and the word rendered "mind" does not mean another part of human nature, but the whole products of the operations of the heart. The Revised Version renders it by "thought," and that is correct if it be given a wide enough application, so as to include emotions, affections, purposes, as well as "thoughts" in the narrower sense. The whole inner man, in all the extent of its manifold operations, that indwelling peace of God will garrison and guard.

So note, however profound and real that Divine peace is, it is to be enjoyed in the midst of warfare. Quiet is not quiescence. God's peace is not torpor. The man that has it has still to wage continual conflict, and day by day to brace himself anew for the fight. The highest energy of action is the result of the deepest calm of heart; just as the motion of this solid, and, as we feel it to be, immovable world, is far more rapid through the abysses of space, and on its own axis, than any of the motions of the things on its surface. So the quiet heart, "which moveth altogether if it move at all," rests whilst it moves, and moves the more swiftly because of its unbroken repose. That peace of God, which is peace militant, is unbroken amidst the conflicts. The wise old Greeks chose for the goddess of Athens the goddess of Wisdom, and whilst they consecrated to her the olive branch, which is the symbol of peace, they set her image on the Parthenon, helmed and spear-bearing, to defend the peace which she brought to earth. So this heavenly virgin, whom the Apostle personifies here, is the "winged sentry, all skillful in the wars," who enters into our hearts and fights for us to keep us in unbroken peace.

It is possible day by day to go out to toil and care and anxiety and change and suffering and conflict, and yet to bear within our hearts the unalterable rest of God. Deep in the bosom of the ocean, beneath the region where winds howl and billows break, there is calm, but the calm is not stagnation. Each drop from these fathomless abysses may be raised to the surface by the power of the sunbeams, expanded there by their heat, and sent on some beneficent message across the world. So, deep in our hearts, beneath the storm, beneath the raving winds and the curling waves, there may be a central repose, as unlike stagnation as it is unlike tumult; and the peace of God may keep, as a warrior, our hearts and minds in Christ Jesus.

What is the plain English of that metaphor? Just this, that a man who has that peace as his conscious possession is lifted above the temptations that otherwise would drag him away. The full cup, filled with precious wine, has no room in it for the poison that otherwise might be poured in. As Jesus Christ has taught us, there is such a thing as cleansing a heart in some measure, and yet because it is "empty," though it is "swept and garnished," the demons come back again. The best way to be made strong to resist temptation is to be lifted above feeling it to be a temptation by reason of the peace possessed. Oh! if our hearts were filled, as they might be filled, with that Divine repose, do you think that the vulgar, coarse-tasting baits which make our mouths water now would have any power over us? Will a man who bears in his hands jewels of priceless value, and knows them to be such, find much temptation when some bit of imitation stuff, made of colored glass and a tinfoil backing, is presented to him? Will the world draw us away if we are rooted and grounded in the peace of God? Geologists tell us that climates are changed and creatures are killed by the slow variation of level in the earth. If you and I can only heave our lives up high enough, the foul things that live down below will find the air too pure and keen for them, and will die and disappear; and all the vermin that stung and nestled down in the flats will be gone when we get up to the heights. The peace of God will keep hearts and their thoughts.

III. Now, lastly, notice how we get the peace of God.

My text is an exuberant promise, but it is knit on to something before by that "and" at the beginning of the verse. It is a promise, as all God's promises are, on conditions. And here are the conditions. "Be careful for nothing; but in everything by prayer and supplication with thanksgiving let your requests be made known unto God." That defines the conditions in part; and the last words of the text itself complete the definition. "In Christ Jesus" describes, not so much where we are to be kept, as a condition under which we shall be. How, then, can I get this peace into my turbulent, changeful life?

I answer, first, trust is peace. It is always so; even when it is misplaced we are at rest. The condition of repose for the human heart is that we shall be "In Christ," who has said, "In the world ye shall have tribulation; [but] in me ye shall have peace." And how may I be "in Him"? Simply by trusting myself to Him. That brings peace with God.

The sinless Son of God has died on the Cross, a sacrifice for the sins of the whole world, for yours and for mine. Let us trust to that and we shall have peace with God, through our Lord Jesus Christ. And "in Him" we have, by trust, inward peace, for He, through our faith, controls our whole natures, and faith leads the lion in a silken leash, like Spenser's Una.

Trust in Christ brings peace amid outward sorrows and conflicts. When the pilot comes on board the captain does not leave the bridge, but stands by the pilot's side. His responsibility is past, but his duties are not over. And when Christ comes into my heart, my effort, my judgment, are not made unnecessary or put on one side. Let Him take the command, and stand beside Him, and carry out His orders, and you will find rest to your souls.

Again, submission is peace. What makes our troubles is not outward circumstances, howsoever afflictive they may be, but the resistance of our spirits to the circumstances. And where a man's will bends and says, "Not mine, but Thine, be done," there is calm. Submission is like the lotion that you apply to the mosquito bites—it takes away the irritation, though the puncture be left. Submission is peace, both as resignation and as obedience.

Communion is peace. You will get no quiet until you live with God. Until he is at your side you will always be moved.

So, dear friends, do you fix this in your minds: a life without Christ is a life without peace. Without Him you may have excitement, pleasure, gratified passions, success, accomplished hopes, but peace never! You never have had it, have you? If you live without Him, you may forget that you have not Him, and you can plunge into the world, and so lose the consciousness of the aching void, but it is there all the same. You never will have peace until you go to Him. There is only one way to get it. The Christless heart is like the troubled sea that cannot rest. There is no peace for it. But in Him you can get it for the asking. "The chastisement of our peace was upon him." For our sakes He died on the Cross, so making peace. Trust Him as your only Hope, Saviour, Friend, and the God of peace will "fill you with all joy and peace in believing." Then bow your wills to Him in acceptance of His providence and in obedience to His commands, and so, "your peace shall be as a river, and your righteousness as the waves of the sea." Then keep your hearts in union and communion with Him, and so His presence will keep you in perfect peace whilst conflicts last, and, with Him at your side, you will pass through the valley of the shadow of death undisturbed, and come to the true Salem, the city of peace, where they beat their swords into ploughshares, and learn and fear war no more.

Almighty Father! Thou seest all our hearts and all our needs, and knowest them better than we, and Thou dost interpret our desires more truly and wisely than we ourselves. We come blessing Thee that we can spread our wants before Thee. Thou lovest Thy children too well to give them the stones that they often ask for, thinking them bread. We would submit ourselves, O Lord! to Thy wise counsel, and accept what Thou dost give, believing that it is for the best. We pray that our hearts may always be kept in the peaceful faith that all things work together for our good if we love God. And we pray that our hearts may more and more be brought under the elevating and calming influence of that Divine love which shall hallow all human affections, and sanctify all duties, and fit us peacefully and joyfully to pass through every vicissitude of life.

Help us to subordinate all other wishes, and treasures, and loves to Thee, and to give our hearts more and more to Thyself. It is only Thou Who canst fill them, and make us blessed, and quiet, and strong. Guide Thou us in all our ways; if to any of us the path is dark, rough, thorny, we beseech Thee that we may have with us the Companion Who makes all paths paths of pleasantness and ways of peace, and that our hearts may burn within us as Jesus Christ walks with us by the way. And on the road, O Lord! help us to think of Thee, to speak to Thee, to do Thy will, and when it pleases Thee, bring us to the home where there is rest. Amen.[2]

---
[2] From *Pulpit Prayers*.

OUR TRUE FRIENDS [1]

If it is true that the river of the water of life, which flows from the throne of God, is the only draught that can ever satisfy the immortal thirst of a soul, then whatever drives me away from the cisterns and to the fountain is on my side. Better to dwell in a dry and thirsty land, where no water is, if it makes me long for the water that rises at the gate of the true Bethlehem, the house of bread, than to dwell in a land flowing with milk and honey, and well-watered in every part. If the cup that I fain would lift to my lips has poison in it, or if its sweetness is making me lose my relish for the pure and tasteless water that flows from the throne of God, there can be no truer friend than that calamity, as men call it, which strikes the cup from my hands, and shivers the glass before I have raised it to my lips. Everything is my friend that helps me toward God.

Everything is my friend that leads me to submission and obedience. The joy of life and the perfection of human nature is an absolutely submitted will, identified with the Divine, both in regard to doing and to enduring. And whatever tends to make my will flexible, so that it corresponds to all the sinuosities, so to speak, of the Divine will, and fits into all its bends and turns, is a blessing to me.

> Our wills are ours, we know not how;
> Our wills are ours, to make them Thine.

[1] From *Similes and Figures from Alexander Maclaren*, by Francis E. Clark. Copyright, 1910, by Fleming H. Revell, and reprinted by permission.

14. THE GUIDING PILLAR [1]

"So it was alway; the cloud covered [the tabernacle] by day, and the appearance of fire by night." Num. 9:16.

The children of Israel in the wilderness, surrounded by miracle, had nothing which we do not possess. They had some things in an inferior form; their sustenance came by manna; ours comes by God's blessing on our daily work, which is better. Their guidance came by this supernatural pillar; ours comes by the reality of which that pillar was nothing but a picture. And so, instead of fancying that men thus led were in advance of us, we should learn that these, the supernatural manifestations, visible and palpable, of God's presence and guidance were the beggarly elements: "God having provided some better thing for us, that they without us should not be made perfect."

With this explanation of the relation between the miracle and symbol of the old, and the reality and standing miracle of the new covenants, let us look at the eternal truths, which are set before us in a transitory form, in this cloud by day and fiery pillar by night.

I. Note, first, the double form of the guiding pillar.

The fire was the center; the cloud was wrapped around it. The former was the symbol, making visible to a generation who had to be taught through their senses the inaccessible holiness, and flashing brightness, and purity of the Divine nature; the latter tempered and veiled the too great brightness for feeble eyes.

The same double element is found in all God's manifestations of Himself to men. In every form of revelation are present both the heart and core of light, which no eye can look upon, and the merciful veil which, because it veils, unveils; because it hides, reveals; makes visible because it conceals; and shows God because it is the hiding of His power.

---
[1] From *The Unchanging Christ*, Alexander & Shepheard (London), 1889.

So, through all the history of His dealings with men, there has ever been what is called in Scripture language the "face," or the "name of God"; the aspect of the Divine nature on which eye can look; and manifested through it there has always been the depth and inaccessible abyss of that infinite Being. We have to be thankful that in the cloud is the fire, and that round the fire is the cloud. For only so can our eyes behold and our hands grasp the else invisible and remote central Sun of the universe. God hides to make better known the glories of His character. His revelation is the flashing of the uncreated and intolerable light of His infinite Being through the encircling clouds of human conceptions and words, or of deeds which each show forth, in forms fitted to our apprehension, some fragment of His luster. After all revelation, He remains unrevealed. After ages of showing forth His glory He is still the King invisible, whom no man hath seen at any time nor can see. The revelation which He makes of Himself is "truth, and is no lie." The recognition of the presence in it of both the fire and the cloud does not cast any doubt on the reality of our imperfect knowledge, or the authentic participation in the nature of the central light, of the sparkles of it which reach us. We know with a real knowledge what we know of Him. What He shows us is Himself, though not His whole self.

This double aspect of all possible revelation of God, which was symbolized in comparatively gross external form in the pillar that led Israel on its march, and lay stretched out and quiescent, a guarding covering above the tabernacle when the weary march was still, recurs all through the history of Old Testament revelation by type, and prophecy, and ceremony, in which the encompassing cloud was comparatively dense, and the light which pierced it relatively faint. It reappears in both elements, but combined in new proportions, so as that "the veil—that is to say, His flesh" is thinned to transparency and all aglow with the indwelling luster of manifest Deity. So a light, set in some fair alabaster vase, shines through its translucent walls, bringing out every delicate tint and meandering vein of color, while itself diffused and softened by the enwrapping medium which it beautifies by passing through its pure walls. Both are made visible and attractive to dull eyes by the conjunction. He that hath seen Christ hath seen the Father, and he that hath seen the Father in Christ hath seen the man Christ as none see Him who are blind to the incarnate Deity which illuminates the manhood in which it dwells.

But we have to note also the varying appearance of the pillar according to need. There was a double change in the pillar according to the hour, and according as the congregation was on the march or encamped. By day it was a cloud; by night it glowed in the darkness. On the march it moved before them, an upright pillar, as gathered together for energetic movement; when the camp rested it "returned to the many thousands of Israel" and lay quietly stretched above the tabernacle like one of the long-drawn motionless clouds above the setting summer's sun, glowing through all its substance with unflashing radiance reflected from unseen light, and "on all the glory" (shrined in the Holy Place beneath) was "a defense."

But these changes of aspect symbolize for us the reality of the Protean capacity of change according to our ever-varying needs, which for our blessing we may find in that ever-changing, unchanging Divine presence which will be our companion, if we will.

It was not only by a natural process that, as daylight declined, what had seemed but a column of smoke, in the fervid desert sunlight, brightened into a column of fire, blazing amid the clear stars. But we may well believe in an actual admeasurement of the degree of light correspondent to the darkness and to the need for certitude and cheering sense of God's protection which the defenseless camp would feel as they lay down to rest.

When the deceitful brightness of earth glistens and dazzles around me, my vision of Him may be "a cloudy screen to temper the deceitful ray"; and when "there stoops on our path, in storm and shade, the frequent night," as earth grows darker, and life becomes grayer and more somber, and verges to its even, the pillar blazes brighter before the weeping eye, and draws near to the lonely heart. We have a God that manifests Himself in the pillar of cloud by day, and in the flaming fire by night.

II. Note the guidance of the pillar.

When it lifts the camp marches; when it glides down and lies motionless the march is stopped and the tents are pitched. The main thing which is dwelt upon in this description of the God-guided pilgrimage of the wandering people is the absolute uncertainty in which they were kept as to the duration of their encampment, and as to the time and circumstances of their march. Sometimes the cloud tarried upon the tabernacle many days; sometimes for a night only; sometimes it lifted in the night. "Whether it was by day or by night that the cloud was taken up, they journeyed. Or whether it were two days, or a month, or a year, that the cloud tarried upon the tabernacle, remaining thereon, the children of Israel abode in their tents, and journeyed not: but when it was taken up, they journeyed." So never, from moment to moment, did they know when the moving cloud might settle, or the resting cloud might soar. Therefore, absolute uncertainty as to the next stage was visibly represented before them by that hovering guide which determined everything, and concerning whose next movement they knew absolutely nothing.

Is not that all true about us? We have no guiding cloud like this. So much the better. Have we not a more real guide? God guides us by circumstances; God guides us by His word; God guides us by His Spirit, speaking through our common sense and in our understanding; and, most of all, God guides us by that dear Son of His, in whom is the fire and round whom is the cloud. And perhaps we may even suppose that our Lord implies some allusion to this very symbol in His own great words, "I am the light of the world; he that followeth me shall not walk in darkness, but shall have the light of life." For the conception of "following" the light seems to make it plain that our Lord's image is not that of the sun in the heavens, or any such supernal light, but of some light that comes near enough to a man to move before him, and behind which he can march. So, I think that Christ Himself laid His hand upon this ancient symbol, and in these great words said in effect, "I am that which it only shadowed and foretold." At all events, whether in them He was pointing to our text or no, we must feel that He is the reality which was expressed by this outward symbol. And no man who can say, "Jesus Christ is the Captain of my salvation, and after His pattern I march; at the pointing of His guiding finger I move; and in His footsteps, He being my helper, I want to tread," need feel or fancy that any possible pillar, floating before the dullest eye, was a better, surer, and Diviner guide than he possesses. They whom Christ guides want none other for leader, pattern, counselor, companion, reward. This Christ is our Christ forever and ever; He will be our guide, even unto death, and beyond it. The pillar that we follow, which will glow with the ruddy flame of love in the darkest hours of life—blessed be His name—will glide in front of us through the valley of the shadow of death, brightest then when the murky midnight is blackest. Nor will the pillar which guides us cease to blaze as did the guide of the desert march, when Jordan has been crossed. It will still move before us on paths of continuous and ever-increasing approach to infinite perfection. They who follow Christ afar off and with faltering steps here shall there "follow the Lamb whithersoever he goeth."

In like manner, the same absolute uncertainty which was intended to keep the Israelites (though it failed often) in the attitude of constant dependence, is the condition in which we all have to live, though we mask it from ourselves. That we do not know what lies before us is a commonplace. The same long tracks of monotonous continuance in the same place and doing the same duties, befall us that befell these men. Years pass, and the pillar spreads itself out, a defense above the unmoving sanctuary. And then, all of a flash, when we are least thinking of change, it gathers itself together, is a pillar again, shoots upwards, and moves forwards; and it is for us to go after it. And so our lives are shuttlecocked between uniform sameness which may become mechanical monotony, and agitation by change which may make us lose our hold of fixed principles and calm faith, unless we recognize that the continuance and the change are alike the will of the guiding God whose will is signified by the stationary or moving pillar.

III. That leads me to the last thing that I would note—viz., the docile following of the Guide.

In the context the writer does not seem to be able to get away from the thought that whatever the pillar did, that moment prompt obedience follows. He says it over and over and over again. "As long as the cloud abode . . . they rested. . . . And when the cloud tarried long . . . [they] journeyed not"; and "when the cloud was a few days on the tabernacle . . . they abode"; and "according to the commandment they journeyed"; and "when the cloud abode until the morning . . . they journeyed"; and "whether it were two days, or a month, or a year, that the cloud tarried . . . [they] journeyed not, but abode in their tents." So, after he has reiterated the thing half a dozen times or more, he finishes by putting it all again in one verse, as the last impression which he would leave from the whole narrative—"at the commandment of the Lord they rested in their tents, and at the commandment of the Lord they journeyed." Obedience was prompt; whensoever and for whatsoever the signal was given the men were ready. In the night, after they had had their tents pitched for a long period, somewhere or other, in the night, when only the watchers' eyes were open, the pillar lifts, and in an instant the alarm is given, and all the camp is in a bustle. That is what we have to set before us as the type of our lives—that we shall be as ready for every indication of God's will as they were. The peace and blessedness of our lives largely depend on our being eager to obey, and therefore quick to perceive the slightest sign of motion in the resting or of rest in the moving pillar which regulates our march and our encamping.

What do we want in order to cultivate and keep such a disposition? We need perpetual watchfulness lest the pillar should lift unnoticed. When Nelson was second in command at Copenhagen, the admiral in command of the fleet hoisted the signal for recall, and Nelson put his telescope to his blind eye and said, "I do not see it." That is very like what we are tempted to do; the signal for unpleasant duties that we want to get out of is hoisted; we are very apt to put the telescope to the blind eye and pretend to ourselves that we do not see the fluttering flags.

We need still more to keep our wills in absolute suspense, if His will has not declared itself. Do not let us be in a hurry to run before God. When the Israelites were crossing the Jordan they were told to leave a great space between themselves and the guiding ark, that they might know how to go, because "they had not passed that way heretofore." Impatient hurrying at God's heels is apt to lead us astray. Let Him get well in front, that you may be quite sure which way He wants you to go, before you go. And if you are not sure which way He wants you to go, be sure that He does not at that moment want you to go anywhere.

We need to hold the present with a slack hand, so as to be ready to fold our tents and take to the road if God will. We must not reckon on continuance, nor strike our roots so deep that it needs a hurricane to remove us. To those who set their gaze on Christ, no present from which He wishes them to remove can be so good for them as the new conditions into which He would have them pass. It is hard to leave the spot, though it be in the desert, where we have so long encamped that it has come to look like home. We may look with regret on the circle of black ashes on the sand where our little fire glinted cheerily, and our feet may ache and our hearts ache more as we begin our tramp once again, but we must set ourselves to meet the God-appointed change cheerfully, in the confidence that nothing will be left behind which it is not good to lose, nor anything met which does not bring a blessing, however its first aspect may be—harsh or sad.

We need, too, to cultivate the habit of prompt obedience. "I made haste and delayed not to keep Thy commandments" is the only safe motto. It is reluctance which usually puts the drag on. Slow obedience is often the germ of incipient disobedience. In matters of prudence and of intellect second thoughts are better than first, and third thoughts, which often come back to first ones, better than second; but, in matters of duty, first thoughts are generally best. They are the instructive response of conscience to the voice of God, while second thoughts are too often the objections of disinclination, or sloth, or cowardice. It is easiest to do our duty when we are first sure of it. It then comes with an impelling power which carries us over obstacles on the crest of a wave, while hesitation and delay leave us stranded in shoal water. If we would follow the pillar, we must follow it at once.

A heart that waits and watches for God's direction, that uses common sense as well as faith to unravel small and great perplexities, and is willing to sit loose to the present, however pleasant, in order that it may not miss the indications which say "Arise! this is not your rest"—fulfills the conditions on which, if we keep them, we may be sure that He will guide us by the right way, and bring us at last to the city of habitation.

Lift our hearts, O Lord! we beseech Thee, to Thyself now; and if there be anything in us that draws a veil between us and Thee, help us to put it away if it is our fault, and do Thou take it away if it is beyond our power. If care or sorrow, joy or sin, are between us and Thee, help us to leave all these behind and beneath us, and to come into blessed and quiet touch with God. And we pray that Thou wouldst strengthen each of us, not only in our hour of public and formal worship, but in all the moments of the day, that God may be in them all, and we may be in God. Compass us about, we pray Thee, with that strengthening and blessed assurance of Thy presence and Thy help; and speak Thy gracious words—which it is impossible for human lips to utter—in the depths of each heart.

We beseech Thee that Thy blessing may, in like manner, attend all assemblies of Thy saints. Bring us all more closely together, teach us to depend more upon the one common Lord, and to fight more bravely for the one Captain. Let Thy life be manifested more and more in all our churches, and may we be able, in our various degrees, and as Thy providence opens to us opportunities, to live witnessing for Jesus Christ our Saviour.

Speak through us so that we may all hear; and let Thy Name be glorified through all our worship this day, for our Saviour Jesus Christ's sake. Amen.[2]

---

[2] From *Pulpit Prayers*.

THE MEASURE OF MIGHT [1]

There is the measure. There is no limit except the uncounted wealth of His own self-manifestation, the flashing light of revealed Divinity. Whatsoever there is of splendor in that, whatsoever there is of power there, in these and in nothing on this side of them lies the limit of the possibilities of a Christian life. Of course there is a working limit at each moment, and that is our capacity to receive, but that capacity varies, may vary indefinitely, may become greater and greater beyond our count or measurement. Our hearts may be more and more capable of God; and in the measure of which they are capable of Him they shall be filled by Him. A limit which is always shifting is no limit at all. A kingdom, the boundaries of which are not the same from one year to another by reason of its own inherent expansive power, may be said to have no fixed limit. And so we appropriate and enclose, as it were, within our own little fence, a tiny portion of the great prairie that rolls boundlessly to the horizon. But tomorrow we may enclose more, if we will, and more and more; and so ever onwards, for all that is God's is ours, and He has given us His whole self to use and to possess through our faith in His Son. A thimble can only take up a thimbleful of the ocean, but what if the thimble be endowed with a power of expansion which has no term known to men? May it not, then, be that some time or other it shall be able to hold so much of the infinite depth as now seems a dream too audacious to be realized?

[1] From *Similes and Figures from Alexander Maclaren*, by Francis E. Clark. Copyright, 1910, by Fleming H. Revell, and reprinted by permission.

15. THE SINGERS BY THE SEA [1]

"And I saw as it were a sea of glass mingled with fire: and them that had gotten the victory over the beast, and over his image, and over his mark, and over the number of his name, stand on the sea of glass, having the harps of God. And they sing the song of Moses the servant of God, and the song of the Lamb." Rev. 15:2, 3.

This vision owes its form partly to the circumstances of the seer and partly to an Old Testament reference. As to the former, John's exile in Patmos occasions unusually numerous allusions to the sea, in this Book of the Revelation. The voice of the glorified Redeemer, for instance, reminds him of the thunder of the waves on the rocky coast. The mysterious Beast rises from its abysses, which might hide so much that was foul and strange. Babylon sinks in ruin, like a millstone tossed by an angel's hand into the sea. And when the vision of the new heavens and the new earth dawns, one of its characteristics is, "there shall be no more sea," the emblem of estrangement, of rebellious power, of futile effort.

Similarly in this vision, the glassy sea shot with fire is but a photograph of what was often seen from John's rocky islet on some still morning when the sunrise "came blushing o'er the sea," or on some evening when the wind dropped, and the flaming west dyed the watery plain with a fading splendor.

Then, as to the other element which colors the representation here, we cannot fail to see that there is an allusion to the Song of Miriam, sung on the banks of the Red Sea, when Pharaoh and his host were buried in the mighty waters. There, as here, the singers stand on the safe shore; there, as here, they hymn a destruction which opened the way to emancipation and joy. The allusion is underlined, as it were, in

---
[1] From *Last Sheaves,* American Tract Society, 1904. Reprinted by permission.

the declaration that the Song which here is sung is "the Song of Moses . . . and of the Lamb."

Now, of course, we cannot use highly imaginative representations, like that of my text, as if they were dogmatic statements, and we have to be very careful in deducing any inferences from such figurative language as this. But still, making all allowance for that, we may gather lessons that may be of use to us. We have here brought before us the victorious choir, their place by the glassy sea, and their triumphant song.

I. The victorious choir.

The description of these jubilant singers is very striking. "They that had gotten the victory over," or, as the original is presented in the Revised Version, "they that had come victorious from"—and it would have been even better to have *out of* than *from*—"the beast, and his image and his mark, and the number of his name." They were conquerors who had fought their way out of a certain tyrannical dominion, and had emerged into freedom. Now, I shall not spend time in the discussions which have been very fascinating to many people, and do not seem to me to have been of much use to anybody, as to whether this "Beast" represents a person, and if so whether it is Nero, or whether it is some unknown and still future individual embodiment of certain tendencies. Never mind about that. The important question is, what made the "beast" a beast?

Well—bestiality, to begin with; which, being turned into modern English, is sensuous animalism. Man is poised in the midst, between two orders of being—if I may use the word "order" in reference to one of them—and he may rise or he may sink. He may go up to the level of Divinity; he may come down to the level of bestiality. And if he does not do the one, he will do the other. You have only to look round you today to see the animal beneath a great deal of the veneer of civilization and refinement in modern society. The unblushing sensuality, or if I may not use that word, I may at least say sensuousness, of many modern ideals in art, in literature, in daily life—what is it but the beast in the man coming to be predominant? How much that is unblushingly practiced, and even defended and applauded, is really giving a free hand to the Sensuous, which ought never to get a free hand, letting the mutineers come up on deck and take command of helm and sextant, flinging the reins on the neck of the steeds, which do noble work when they are well held in, but set the heavens on fire, like Phaeton's team, when they are allowed their way. There are other aspects of what make the Beast a beast. I put them all in two words, God-forgetting selfishness and God-defying opposition of will against Christ. If you take the context you will find, amidst a great deal that is very difficult to understand, this one thing emphasized, that the Beast and the Lamb divide the world between them, and that whoever is not on the side of the one is on the side of the other. Under which King? Who is *your* Lord and Master? You young people especially, are you going to serve the flesh, or are you going to put your heel on the neck of the brute, and live for the God whom you may bring to dwell within you? Which are you doing?

The next point is that the dominion of this "Beast," which is shorthand for all the lower and animal tendencies, is an established fact, out of which a man has to fight his way. "They have gotten the victory *out of* the beast . . . and the number of his name." There is nothing in this world worth the having and the being, which is not the result of a deadly earnest fight. If you make up your minds, or if without ever having had the courage to make them up, you let yourselves drift into the position of taking up the line of least resistance and doing what is easiest, then your fate is settled, and down you will go. I do not mean in regard to outward things. You may prosper in them, and win wealth or fame if your aims go in that direction, but in regard to the true aims of life, unless you are prepared to fight, you will be a poor creature whilst you live, and a wreck altogether when you come to die. They "got the victory out of the beast"; plucked it from the very jaws of the brute; and that is what we have to do. As the good old-fashioned hymn says:

> Now we must fight if we would reign;
> Increase our courage, Lord.

But there is one more thing to note about these victorious choristers. How did they get the victory? There is only one answer to that question—because they joined themselves to the Victor-Lamb. It is a strange paradox that runs through this Book of the Revelation, that, as I have already suggested, the Lamb is pitted against the Beast; and with entire destruction of the verisimilitude of the metaphor, the Lamb is made to be a Warrior-Lamb, Who "goes forth"—strange as it sounds—"conquering, and to conquer." That covers a deep truth. Christ cures the animalism of humanity by His sacrifice on the Cross, and by His meekness and gentleness. And if you are ever to overcome your worse self, and to have any share in that jubilant song of triumph at the last, I believe in my heart of hearts that the only way by which you can do so is by trusting yourselves to Him Who "teaches our hands to war and our fingers to fight."

When He said to us, "be of good cheer; I have overcome the world," He implied that "this is the victory that"—for us—"overcometh the world, even our faith," by which we unite ourselves with Him, participating by derivation in His victorious power, and, therefore, are "more than conquerors through him that loved us." They have "gotten the victory from the beast." Let me beseech you to fight under the same Leader and with the same weapons as they did, or the Beast will gain dominion over you.

And now turn to the second point—

II. The glassy sea by which the victors stood.

Of course, the allusion to the story in Exodus and the propriety of the picture, make it necessary that we should suppose that they who stand "on the sea of glass" are not represented as if they had their feet planted on its calm surface, but that "on" here means "above," "by the side of," on the safe shore, with the glassy sea stretching in front of them. Now this sea of glass, by which these victors stood, has appeared already in this book, where it is represented as lying placid and even before the Divine Throne. I suppose that both there and in our text, it represents by a very natural metaphor the aggregate of the Divine dealings and self-manifestations to men; on whose calm surface, if I may so say, as on a great, shining mirror, the throne of God and He who sits upon it, are in some degree reflected. One of the psalms has the same idea, in a somewhat different form, when it says, "Thy way is in the sea, and thy path in the deep waters, and thy footsteps are not known." Another psalm echoes the thought when it says, "Thy judgments are a mighty deep." And one of the Apostles winds up his discussion about the mysteries of the kingdom of God with, "Oh! the depth of the riches of the wisdom and knowledge of God. How unsearchable are His judgments." So I suppose we may consider that it is in accordance with the analogy of Scripture, as well as with the natural propriety of the symbolism, if we see, in this sea of glass mingled with fire, an emblem of the whole dealings of God with man, through which are ever and anon shot, as it were, fiery streaks, like the scarlet threads in Venetian glass.

This noble symbol carries with it some great and precious thoughts. That sea is transparent. It is deep, but it is not dark by reason of mud, but by reason of its clear translucent depth; and when vision fails, it is not because of obscuration there, but of our weak sight. I have seen a like sea, without a speck of mire or dirt and with no weed on its margin, rising and falling on marble cliffs that it had polished into discovery of their golden veins. Such is this "glassy sea," pure and clean. "The judgments of the Lord are true and righteous altogether." We know their motives and purposes; they come from Love; they tend towards man's perfecting. And if, at any time, it is difficult to hold fast by that belief as to their origin because of their complexity, or difficult to see how they tend to that issue, still, as does the psalm to which I have already referred, we have to link together the two conceptions: "Thy way is in the sea" and "Thy way is in the sanctuary."

Again, the sea of glass was calm and stable. To us, tossing upon it, it often looks tempestuous enough. To them, looking down from above, it is smoothed into a watery plain, a glassy mirror. That crystal sea was shot with fire. The judgments of God necessarily are sometimes punitive, retributive, destructive, but they that are in sympathy with the Lamb, and have shaken off the tyranny of the Beast, in the measure in which they have done so, even here and now see in them, and understand, "the loving-kindness of the Lord" even when He smites.

And so I come to the last point—

III. The song of this victorious choir.

I do not attempt to expound it. I simply wish to draw attention to its central thought. These conquering choristers stand, like Miriam and her maiden band with their timbrels, on the safe shore, and as they look out on the calm waters that have buried Pharaoh and his hosts, they lift up their song of praise, because of the destructive judgments that have led to liberty. The gist of their song is this, that God's dealings with man—the transparent crystal and the fiery streaks—alike are the outcome of His righteous love, and alike are intended to lead men to know and worship Him. Even when there come "terrible things in righteousness" to the world, or to us individually, if we are wedded to Jesus Christ they will yield to us here, and far more clearly and continuously hereafter, occasions for thankfulness, for praise, for clear perception of the Divine character, and for more lowly worship at His feet. "When the wicked perish there is shouting," says Proverbs. And when God, as is sometimes the case, comes forth and smites into dust some hoary institution that has been the source of miseries to mankind, then men ought to rejoice, and, in spite of sympathy and compassion, ought to feel that God has done a mighty thing in mercy, though mercy had an envelope of wrath. There is nothing of the weak sentimentality which characterizes some people's theories in the New Testament conception of God. He is the God of love, but His very love must sometimes nerve His arm to strike, and sharpen His spear to slay.

Let us remember that that is true about our individual lives. Let us take our place where the choristers stand by the glassy sea, in so far as we can do so here and now. Let us recognize habitually, that even the retributive and destructive and afflictive acts of God come forth from His righteousness and for our good, and we shall be less astonished when the bitter draught comes to our lips, and be able to say, even whilst we take it: "The cup which my Father hath given me, shall I not drink it?" And afterwards we shall stand like the harpers by the glassy sea, and praise Him for our sorrows, our losses, our pains; and for all the way by which the Lord our God hath led us. . .

So let us acquiesce in present imperfect knowledge, and not be in too great a hurry to pronounce, with our fallible judgment and our partial information as to a half-finished process, what is in accordance with, and what is contrary to, the Divine nature. Abraham had the boldness to say: "Shall not the Judge of all the earth do right?"—which did not mean "I will acquiesce in His acts, though I cannot see their righteousness, because He did them"; but did mean: "Men have a standard of right and wrong to which they expect that the Divine acts will conform." That is true, no doubt, but it is a principle that has to be very cautiously applied, for the reasons just stated. We see but a small segment of the circle here, and our judgment of it had best be suspended till we see the perfect round. We shall be most modest and wise if we "judge nothing before the time." But we can confidently accept Christ's promise: "What thou knowest not now; thou shalt know hereafter." Since we may hope to join the victorious choristers by the sea of glass, let us not contradict our future song of praise by our present murmurings and complaints.

Brethren, this vision shows us, too, the path of victory. Take Jesus Christ for your captain, and in His strength fight, and He will bring you at last to the eternal shore; and as the unsetting sun rises, it will touch with golden beams the calm ocean, beneath which the oppressors lie buried for ever. If we let the Beast write his name on our foreheads, we shall sink with him in the mighty waters. If we take the Lamb first for our sacrifice, and then for our King, He will break the yoke of bondage from off our necks, and bring us at last to the safe beach, and put a new song into our mouths, of praise to Him Who has gotten us the victory "over the beast . . . and the number of his name."

O Lord! Thy glory fills the heavens, and the earth is full of Thy goodness. We bow before Thee with lowly voices and our humble praise, which yet we believe is pleasant in Thine ear, and blends with the song of the seraphs. Truly Thou art high above all our creatural limitations and weakness, separate from us, and yet how near Thou art. How Thy love has passed the gulf between us, and would draw us to cross it, and to come into fellowship and closest touch with Thee. We thank Thee that we can come so near to Thee, and that in the narrow room of our hearts Thou wilt dwell, and abide with us if we are humble and of a contrite spirit.

Help us, we pray Thee, to understand the loving-kindness of the Lord; and if ever Thy judgments seem to us a mighty deep which we have no plummets to fathom, nor eyes to scrutinize, may we rejoice in that righteousness which is as a great mountain whose roots are beneath the abyss. Do Thou lift upon us the light of Thy countenance, and help us to enter into the secret place of the Most High, and there may we find the beauty of the Lord, and inquire in His Temple. Through Jesus Christ our Lord and Saviour. Amen.[2]

---
[2] From *Pulpit Prayers*.

USING OUR RESOURCES [1]

Be sure that to its last particle you are using the strength you have, ere you complain of not having enough for your tasks. Take heed of the vagrant expectations that wait for they know not what, and the apparent prayers that are really substitutes for possible service. "Why liest thou on thy face? Speak unto the children of Israel that they go forward." But go out among the crowds, and give confidently what you have, and you will find that you have enough and to spare. If ever our stores seem inadequate, it is because they are reckoned up by sense, which takes cognizance of the visible, instead of faith which beholds the real. Certainly five loaves and two small fishes are not enough, but are not five loaves and two small fishes and a miracle-working hand behind them, enough? It is poor calculation that leaves out Christ from the estimate of our forces. The weakest man and Jesus to back him are more than all antagonism, more than sufficient for all duty. Be not seduced into doubt of your power, or of your success, by others' sneers, or by your own faintheartedness. The confidence of ability is ability. "Screw your courage to the sticking place, and you will not fail"—and see to it that you use the resources you have, as good stewards of the manifold grace of God. "Put on thy strength, O Zion."

[1] From *Similes and Figures from Alexander Maclaren,* by Francis E. Clark. Copyright, 1910, by Fleming H. Revell, and reprinted by permission.

16. ITTAI OF GATH [1]

"And Ittai answered the king, and said, As the Lord liveth, and as my lord the king liveth, surely in what place my lord the king shall be, whether in death or life, even there also will thy servant be."
II SAM. 15:21.

It was the darkest hour in David's life. No more pathetic page is found in the Old Testament than that which tells the story of his flight before Absalom. He is crushed by the consciousness that his punishment is deserved—the bitter fruit of the sin that filled all his later life with darkness. His courage and his buoyancy have left him. He has no spirit to make a stand or strike a blow. If Shimei runs along the hillside abreast of him, shrieking curses as he goes, all he says is: "Let him curse; for the Lord hath bidden him."

So, heartbroken and spiritless, he leaves Jerusalem. And as soon as he has got clear of the city he calls a halt, in order that he may muster his followers and see on whom he may depend. Foremost among the little band come six hundred men from Gath—Philistines—from Goliath's city. These men, singularly enough, the king had chosen as his bodyguard; perhaps he was not altogether sure of the loyalty of his own subjects, and possibly felt safer with foreign mercenaries, who could have no secret leanings to the deposed house of Saul. Be that as it may, the narrative tells us that these men had "come after him from Gath." He had been there twice in the old days in his flight from Saul, and the second visit had extended over something more than a year. Probably during that period his personal attraction, and his reputation as a brilliant leader, had led these rough soldiers to attach themselves to his service, and to be ready to forsake home and kindred in order to fight beside him.

---
[1] From *Christ in the Heart,* Hodder & Stoughton Ltd. (London). Reprinted by permission.

At all events here they are, "faithful among the faithless" as foreign soldiers surrounding a king often are—notably, for instance, the Swiss guard in the French Revolution. Their strong arms might have been of great use to David, but his generosity cannot think of involving them in his fall, and so he says to them: "I am not going to fight; I have no plan. I am going where I can. You go back and 'worship the rising sun.' Absalom will take you and be glad of your help. And as for me, I thank you for your past loyalty. Mercy and peace be with you!"

It is a beautiful nature that in the depth of sorrow shrinks from dragging other people down with itself. Generosity breeds generosity, and the Philistine captain breaks out into a burst of passionate devotion, garnished, in soldier-fashion, with an unnecessary oath or two, but ringing very sincere and meaning a great deal. As for himself and his men, they have chosen their side. Whoever goes, they stay. Whatever befalls, they stick by David; and if the worst comes to the worst they can all die together, and their corpses lie in firm ranks round about their dead king. David's heart is touched and warmed by their outspoken loyalty; he yields and accepts their service. Ittai and his noble six hundred tramp on, out of our sight, and all their households behind them. Now what is there, in all that, to make a sermon out of?

I. First, look at the picture of that Philistine soldier, as teaching us what grand passionate self-sacrifice may be evolved out of the roughest natures.

Analyze his words, and do you not hear, ringing in them, these three things, which are the seed of all nobility and splendor in human character? First, a passionate personal attachment; then, that love, issuing as such love always does, in willing sacrifice that recks not for a moment of personal consequences; that is ready to accept anything for itself if it can serve the object of its devotion, and will count life well expended if it is flung away in such a service. And we see, lastly, in these words a supreme restful delight in the presence of him whom the heart loves. For Ittai and his men, the one thing needful was to be beside him in whose eye they had lived, from whose presence they had caught inspiration; their trusted leader, before whom their souls bowed down. So then his vehement speech is the pure language of love.

Now these three things—a passionate personal attachment, issuing in spontaneous heroism of self-abandonment, and in supreme satisfaction in the beloved presence—may spring up in the rudest, roughest nature. A Philistine soldier was not a very likely man in whom to find refined and lofty emotion. He was hard by nature, hardened by his rough trade, and unconscious that he was doing anything at all heroic or great.

Something had smitten this rock, and out of it there came the pure refreshing stream. And so I say to you, the weakest and the lowest, the roughest and the hardest, the most selfishly absorbed man and woman among us, has lying in him and her dormant capacities for flaming up into such a splendor of devotion and magnificence of heroic self-sacrifice as is represented in these words of my text.

A mother will do it for her child, and never think that she has done anything extraordinary; husbands will do such things for wives; wives for husbands; friends and lovers for one another. All who know the sweetness and power of the bond of affection know that there is nothing more gladsome than to fling one's self away for the sake of those whom we love. And the capacity for such love and sacrifice lies in all of us, prosaic, commonplace people as we are, with no great field on which to work out our heroisms; yet it is in us to love and give ourselves away thus if once the heart be stirred.

And lastly, this capacity which lies dormant in all of us, if once it is roused to action will make a man blessed and dignified as nothing else will. The joy of unselfish love is the purest joy that man can taste; the joy of perfect self-sacrifice is the highest joy that humanity can possess; and they lie open for us all.

And wherever, in some humble measure, these emotions of which I have been speaking are realized, there you get weakness springing up into strength, and the ignoble into loftiness. Astronomers tell us that, sometimes, a star that has shone inconspicuous, and stood low down in their catalogues as of fifth or sixth magnitude, will all at once flame out, having kindled and caught fire somehow, and will blaze in the heavens, outshining Jupiter and Venus. And so some poor, vulgar, narrow nature, touched by the Promethean fire of pure love that leads to perfect sacrifice, will "flame in the forehead of the morning sky," an undying splendor, and a light forevermore.

Brethren! My appeal to you is a very plain and simple one, founded on these facts: You have all that capacity in you, and you are all responsible for the use of it. What have you done with it? Is there any person or thing in this world that has ever been able to lift you up out of your miserable selves? Is there any magnet that has proved strong enough to raise you from the low levels along which your life creeps? Have you ever known the thrill of resolving to become the bondservant and the slave of some great cause not your own? Or are you, as so many of you are, like spiders living in the midst of your web, mainly intent upon what you can catch in it? You have these capacities slumbering in you. Have you ever set a light to that inert mass of enthusiasm that lies in you? Have you ever waked up the sleeper? Look at this rough soldier of my text, and learn from him the lesson that there is nothing that so ennobles and dignifies a commonplace nature as enthusiasm for a great cause, or self-sacrificing love for a worthy heart.

II. The second remark which I make is this: These possibilities of love and sacrifice point plainly to God in Christ as their true object. "Whose image and superscription hath it?" said Christ, looking at the Roman *denarius* that they brought and laid on His palm. If the Emperor's head is on it, why, then, *he* has a right to it as tribute. And then he went on to say, "Render therefore unto Caesar the things which are Caesar's; and unto God the things that are God's." So there are things that have God's image and superscription stamped on them, and such are our hearts, our whole constitution and nature. As plainly as the penny had the head of Augustus on it, and therefore proclaimed that he was Emperor where it was current, so plainly does every soul carry in the image of God the witness that He is its owner and that it should be rendered in tribute to Him.

And amongst all these marks of a Divine possession and a Divine destination printed upon human nature, it seems to me that none are plainer than this fact, that we can all of us thus give ourselves away in the abandonment of a profound and all-surrendering love. That capacity unmistakably proclaims that it is destined to be directed toward God and to find its rest in Him. As distinctly as some silver cup, with its owner's initials and arms engraved upon it, declares itself to be "meet for the master's use," so distinctly does your soul, by reason of this capacity, proclaim that it is meant to be turned to Him in Whom alone all love can find its perfect satisfaction; for Whom alone it is supremely blessed and great to shed life itself: and Who only has the authority over our human spirits.

We are made with hearts that need to rest upon an absolute love; we are made with understandings that need to grasp a pure, a perfect, and, as I believe, paradoxical though it may sound, a personal Truth. We are made with wills that crave for an absolute authoritative command, and we are made with a moral nature that needs a perfect holiness. And we need all that love, truth, authority, purity, to be gathered into one, for the misery of the world is that when we set out to look for treasures we have to go into many lands and to many merchants to buy many goodly pearls. But we need One of great price, in which all our wealth may be invested. We need that One to be an undying and perpetual possession. There is One to Whom our love can ever cleave, and fear none of the sorrows or imperfections that make earthward-turned love a rose with many a thorn, One for Whom it is pure gain to lose ourselves, One Who is plainly the only worthy recipient of the whole love and self-surrender of the heart.

That One is God, revealed and brought near to us in Jesus Christ. In that great Saviour we have a love at once Divine and human, we have the great transcendent instance of love leading to sacrifice. On that love and sacrifice for us Christ builds His claim on us for our hearts, and our all. Life alone can communicate life; it is only light that can diffuse light. It is only love that can kindle love; it is only sacrifice that can inspire sacrifice. And so He comes to us, and asks that we should just love Him back again as He has loved us. He first gives Himself utterly for and to us, and then asks us to give ourselves wholly to Him. He first yields up His own life, and then He says: "He that loseth his life for my sake shall find it." The object, the true object for all this depth of love which lies slumbering in our hearts, is God in Christ, the Christ that died for us.

III. And now, lastly, observe that the terrible misdirection of these capacities is the sin and the misery of the world.

I will not say that such emotions, even when expended on creatures, are ever wasted. For however unworthy may be the objects on which they are lavished, the man himself is the better and the higher for having cherished them. The mother, when she forgets self in her child, though her love and self-forgetfulness and self-sacrifice may, in some respects, be called but an animal instinct, is elevated and ennobled by the exercise of them. The patriot and the thinker, the philanthropist, aye! even— although I take him to be the lowest of the scale—the soldier who, in some cause which he thinks to be a good one, and not merely in the tigerish madness of the battlefield, throws away his life—are lifted in the scale of being by their self-abnegation.

And so I am not going to say that when men love each other passionately and deeply, and sacrifice themselves for one another, or for some cause or purpose affecting only temporal matters, the precious elixir of love is wasted. God forbid! But I do say that all these objects, sweet and gracious as some of them are, ennobling and elevating as some of them are, if they are taken apart from God, are insufficient to fill your hearts; and that if they are slipped in between you and God, as they often are, then they bring sin and sorrow.

There is nothing more tragic in this world than the misdirection of man's capacity for love and sacrifice. It is like the old story in the Book of Daniel, which tells how the heathen monarch made a great feast, and when the wine began to inflame the guests, sent for the sacred vessels taken from the Temple of Jerusalem, that had been used for Jehovah's worship; and (as the narrative says, with a kind of shudder at the profanation) "They brought the golden vessels that were taken out of the temple of the house of God which was at Jerusalem; and the king, and his princes, his wives, and his concubines, drank in them. They drank wine, and praised the gods." So this heart of mine, which, as I said, has the Master's initials and His arms engraven upon it, in token that it is His cup, I too often fill with the poisonous and intoxicating draught of earthly pleasure and earthly affections; and as I drink it, the madness goes through my veins, and I praise gods of my own making instead of Him Whom alone I ought to love.

Ah! brethren, we should be our own rebukes in this matter, and the heroism of the world should put to shame the cowardice and the selfishness of the Church. Contrast the depth of your affection for your household with the tepidity of your love for your Saviour. Contrast the willingness with which you sacrifice yourself for some dear one with the grudgingness with which you yield yourselves to Him. Contrast the rest and the sense of satisfaction in the presence of those you love, and your desolation when they are absent, with the indifference whether you have Christ beside you or not. And remember that the measure of your power of loving is the measure of your obligation to love your Lord; and that if you are all frost to Him and fervor to them, then in a very solemn sense "a man's foes shall be they of his own household." "He that loveth father or mother more than Me is not worthy of Me!"

And so let me gather all that I have been saying into the one earnest beseeching of you that you would bring that power of uncalculating love and self-sacrificing affection which is in you, and would fasten it where it ought to fix—on Christ who died on the Cross for you. Such a love will bring blessedness to you. Such a love will ennoble and dignify your whole nature, and make you a far greater and fairer man or woman than you otherwise ever could be. Like some little bit of black carbon put into an electric current, my poor nature will flame into beauty and radiance when that spark touches it. So love Him and be at peace; give yourselves to Him and He will give you back yourselves, ennobled and transfigured by the surrender. Lay yourselves on His altar, and that altar will sanctify both the giver and the gift. If you can take this rough Philistine soldier's words in their spirit, and in a higher sense, say, "Whether I live, I live unto the Lord, or whether I die, I die unto the Lord; living or dying, I am the Lord's," He will let you enlist in His army; and give you for your marching orders this command and this hope, "If any man serve me, let him follow me; and where I am, there shall also my servant be."

O Lord! we would come to bless Thee with heart and soul and voice, for Thy mercies endure forever, and in their continuance and greatness beggar all our thankfulness. To Thee we turn, O Lord! and in Thy ineffable Name we find all that we need.

O Lord! let Thy gracious presence come to us, and Thy love be upon us. Thou dost brighten the sky with Thy sunshine today; brighten our hearts, we beseech Thee, with the better light of Thy beheld love. May all that is within us bless the Lord, and praise His holy Name.

O Lord! cleanse our hearts, we beseech Thee, take from them all that is unworthy of Thee and contrary to our high calling. May we more and more live as Christ would have lived in our place. May we more and more learn the relative importance of the things temporal and the things eternal. May we be given grace to conquer ourselves, to purify ourselves, perfecting holiness in the fear of the Lord. May we have a growing consciousness that Thou art with us and working on us; and may our profiting appear unto all men, that they may see by our daily lives that we live by a perfect law, and are helped to live by a perfect Spirit.

Hear, and answer us; through Christ our Saviour. Amen.[2]

---
[2] From *Pulpit Prayers*.

KNOWING CHRIST [1]

Do you know Christ as a man knows his friend, or do you know Him as you know about Julius Caesar? Do you know Christ because you live with Him and He with you, or do you know about Him in that fashion in which a man in a great city knows about his neighbor across the street, that has lived beside him for five and twenty years and never spoken to him once all the time? Is that your knowledge of Christ? If so, it is no knowledge at all. "I have heard of Him by the hearing of the ear," describes all the acquaintance which a great many of my friends here have with Him! Oh, my brother! the very fact that He has been so long with you is the reason why you know so little about Him. People that live close to something, which men come from the ends of the earth to see, have often never seen it. A man may have lived all his life within sound of Niagara, and perhaps never have gone to look at the rush of the waters. Is that what you do with Jesus Christ? Are you so accustomed to hear about Him that you do not know Him? Have you so long heard of Him that you never come to see Him? "Have I been so long with you, and yet hast thou not known me?"

[1] From *Similes and Figures from Alexander Maclaren*, by Francis E. Clark. Copyright, 1910, by Fleming H. Revell, and reprinted by permission.

17. CHRIST'S TOUCH [1]

"Jesus . . . put forth His hand, and touched him." MARK 1:41.

"Behold the servant of the Lord" might be the motto of this Gospel, and "He went about doing good, and healing," the summing up of its facts. We have in it comparatively few of our Lord's discourses, none of His longer, and not very many of His briefer ones. It contains but four parables. This Evangelist gives no miraculous birth as in Matthew, no angels adoring there as in Luke, no gazing into the secrets of Eternity, where the Word, Who afterwards became flesh, dwelt in the bosom of the Father, as in John. He begins with a brief reference to the forerunner, and then plunges into the story of Christ's life of service to man, and service for God.

In carrying out his conception the Evangelist omits many things found in the other Gospels, which involve the idea of dignity and dominion, while he adds to the incidents which he has in common with them not a few fine and subtle touches to heighten the impression of our Lord's toil and eagerness in His patient loving service. Perhaps it may be an instance of this that we find more prominence given to our Lord's touch as connected with His miracles than in the other Gospels, or perhaps it may merely be an instance of the vivid portraiture, the result of a keen eye for externals, which is so marked a characteristic of this Gospel. Whatever the reason, the fact is plain, that Mark delights to dwell on Christ's touch.

The instances are these—First, He puts out His hand, and "lifts up" Peter's wife's mother, and immediately the fever left her (1:31); then, unrepelled by the foul disease, He lays His pure hand upon the leper, and the living mass of corruption is healed (1:41); again, He lays His hand on the clammy marble of the dead child's forehead, and she lives (1:41).

---
[1] From *Christ in the Heart*, Hodder & Stoughton Ltd. (London). Reprinted by permission.

Further, we have incidental statement that He was so hindered in His mighty works by unbelief that He could only lay His hands on a few sick folk and heal them (6:5). We find next two remarkable incidents, peculiar to Mark, both like each other and unlike our Lord's other miracles. One is the gradual healing of that deaf and dumb man whom Christ took apart from the crowd, laid His hands on him, thrust His fingers into his ears as if He would clear some impediment, touched his tongue with saliva, said to him, "Be opened"; and the man can hear (7:34). And the other is, the gradual healing of a blind man whom our Lord again leads apart from the crowd, takes by the hand, lays His own kind hands upon the poor sightless eyeballs, and with singular slowness of progress effects a cure, not by a leap and a bound as He generally does, but by steps and stages; tries it once and finds partial success, has to apply the curative process again and then the man can see (8:23). In addition to these instances there are two other incidents which may also be adduced. It is Mark alone who records for us the fact that He took little children in His arms, and blessed them. It is Mark alone who records for us the fact that when He came down from the Mount of Transfiguration He laid His hand upon the demoniac boy, writhing in the grip of his tormentor, and lifted him up.

There is much taught us, if we will patiently consider it, by that touch of Christ's, and I wish to try to bring out its meaning and power.

I. Whatever diviner and sacreder aspect there may be in these incidents, the first thing, and in some senses the most precious thing in them, is that they are the natural expression of a truly human tenderness and compassion.

Now we are so accustomed, and as I believe quite rightly, to look at all Christ's life down to its minutest events as intended to be a revelation of God, that we are sometimes apt to think about it as if his motive and purpose in everything was didactic. So an unreality creeps over our conceptions of Christ's life, and we need to be reminded that He was not always acting and speaking in order to convey instruction, but that words and deeds were drawn from Him by the play of simple human feelings. He pitied not only in order to teach us the heart of God, but because His own man's heart was touched with a feeling of men's infirmities. We are too apt to think of Him as posing before men with the intent of giving the great revelation of the Love of God. It is the love of Christ Himself, spontaneous, instinctive, without the thought of anything but the suffering it sees, which gushes out and leads Him to put forth His hand to the outcast beggars, the blind, the deaf, the lepers. That is the first great lesson we have to learn from this and other stories—the swift human sympathy and heart of grace and tenderness which Jesus Christ had for all human suffering, and has today as truly as ever.

There is more than this instinctive sympathy taught by Christ's touch. But it is distinctly taught. How beautifully that comes out in the story of the leper! That wretched man had long dwelt in his isolation. The touch of a friend's hand or the kiss of loving lips had been long denied him. Christ looks on him, and before he reflects the spontaneous impulse of pity breaks through the barriers of legal prohibitions, and of natural repugnance, and leads Him to lay His holy and healing hand on his foulness.

True pity always instinctively leads us to seek to come near those who are its objects. A man tells his friend some sad story of his sufferings, and while he speaks, unconsciously his listener lays his hand on his arm and, by a silent pressure, tells his sympathy. So Christ did with these men —not only in order that He might reveal God to us, but because He was a man, and therefore felt ere He thought. Out flashed from his heart the swift sympathy, followed by the tender pressure of the loving hand—a hand that tried through flesh to reach spirit and come near the sufferer that it might succor and remove the sorrow.

Christ's pity is shown by His touch to have this true characteristic of true pity, that it overcomes disgust. All real sympathy does that. Christ is not turned away by the shining whiteness of the leprosy, nor by the eating pestilence beneath it; He is not turned away by the clammy marble hand of the poor dead maiden, nor by the fevered skin of the old woman gasping on her pallet. He lays hold on each, the flushed patient, the loathsome leper, the sacred dead, with the all-equalizing touch of a universal love and pity, which disregards all that is repellent and overflows every barrier and pours itself over every sufferer. We have the same pity of the same Christ to trust to and to lay hold of today. He is high above us and yet bending over us; stretching His hand from the throne as truly as He put it out when here on earth; and ready to take us all to His heart, in spite of our weakness and wickedness, our failings and our shortcomings, the fever of our flesh and hearts' desires, the leprosy of our many corruptions, and the death of our sins—and to hold us ever in the strong gentle clasp of His Divine, Omnipotent, and tender hand. This Christ lays hold on us because He loves us, and will not be turned from His compassion by the most loathsome foulness of ours.

II. And now take another point of view from which we may regard this touch of Christ: namely as the medium of His miraculous power.

There is nothing to me more remarkable about the miracles of our Lord than the royal variety of His methods of healing. Sometimes He works at a distance, sometimes He requires, as it would appear for good reasons, the proximity of the person to be blessed. Sometimes He works by a simple word: "Lazarus, come forth!" "Peace, be still!" "Come out of him!"; sometimes by a word and a touch, as in the instances before us; sometimes by a touch without a word; sometimes by a word and a touch and a vehicle, as in the saliva that was put on the tongue, and in the ears of the deaf, and on the eyes of the blind; sometimes by a vehicle without a word, without a touch, without His presence, as when He said "Go, wash in the pool of Siloam! . . . and [he] washed, and was clean." So the Divine worker varies infinitely and at pleasure yet not arbitrarily but for profound, even if not always discoverable, reasons, the methods of His miracle-working power, in order that we may learn by these varieties of ways that He is tied to no way; and that His hand, strong and almighty, uses methods and tosses aside methods according to His pleasure, the methods being vitalized when they are used by His will, and being nothing at all in themselves.

The very variety of His methods, then, teaches us that the true cause in every case is His own bare will. A simple word is the highest and most adequate expression of that will. His word is all powerful; and that is the very signature of divinity. Of Whom has it been true from of old that "He spake, and it was done; he commanded, and it stood fast"? Do you believe in a Christ Whose bare will, thrown among material things, makes them all plastic, as clay in the potter's hands, whose mouth rebukes the demons and they flee, rebukes death and it looses its grasp, rebukes the tempest and there is a calm, rebukes disease and there comes health?

But this use of Christ's touch as apparent means for conveying His miraculous power also serves as an illustration of a principle which is exemplified in all His revelation, namely, the employment in condescension to men's weakness, of outward means as the apparent vehicles of His spiritual power. Just as by the material vehicle sometimes employed for cure, He gave these poor sensebound natures a ladder by which their faith in His healing power might climb, so in the manner of His revelation and communication of His spiritual gifts, there is provision for the wants of us men, who ever need some body for spirit to make itself manifest by, some form for the ethereal reality, some "tabernacle" for the "sun." "Sacraments," outward ceremonies, forms of worship are vehicles which the Divine Spirit uses in order to bring His gifts to the hearts and the minds of men. They are like the touch of the Christ which heals, not by any virtue in itself, apart from His will which chooses to make it the apparent medium of healing. All these externals are nothing, as the pipes of an organ are nothing, until His breath is breathed through them, and then the flood of sweet sound pours out.

Do not despise the material vehicles and the outward helps which Christ uses for the communication of His healing and His life, but remember that the help that is done upon earth, He does it all Himself. Even Christ's touch is nothing, if it were not for His own will which flows through it.

III. Consider Christ's touch as a shadow and symbol of the very heart of His work.

Go back to the past history of this man. Ever since his disease declared itself no human being had touched him. If he had a wife he had been separated from her; if he had children their lips had never kissed his, nor their little hands found their way into his hard palm. Alone he had been walking with the plague-cloth over his face, and the cry "unclean!" on his lips, lest any man should come near him. Skulking in his isolation how he must have hungered for the touch of a hand! Every Jew was forbidden to approach him but the priest, who, if he were cured might pass his hand over the place and pronounce him clean. And here comes a man Who breaks down all the restrictions, stretches a frank hand out across the walls of separation and touches him. What a reviving assurance of love not yet dead, must have come to the man as Christ grasped his hand, even if he saw in him only a stranger who was not afraid of him and did not turn from him!

But besides this thrill of human sympathy, which came hope-bringing to the leper, Christ's touch had much significance, if we remember that, according to the Mosaic legislation, the priest and the priest alone was to lay his hands on the tainted skin and pronounce the leper whole. So Christ's touch was a priest's touch. He lays His hand on corruption and is not tainted. The corruption with which He comes in contact becomes purity. Are not these really the profoundest truths as to His whole work in the world? What is it all but laying hold of the leper and the outcast and the dead—His sympathy leading to His identification of Himself with us in our weakness and misery?

That sympathetic life-bringing touch is put forth once for all in His Incarnation and Death. "He taketh hold of the seed of Abraham," says the Epistle to the Hebrews, looking at our Lord's work under this same metaphor, and explaining that His laying hold of men was His being "made in all points like unto his brethren." Just as he took hold of the fevered woman and lifted her from her bed; or, as He thrust His fingers into the deaf ears of that poor man stopped by some impediment, so in analogous fashion, He becomes one of those whom He would save and help. In His assumption of Humanity and in His bowing of His head to death, we behold Him laying hold of our weakness and entering into the fellowship of our pains and of the fruit of sin.

Just as He touches the leper and is unpolluted, or the fever patient and receives no contagion, or the dead and draws no chill of mortality into His warm hand, so He becomes like His brethren in all things, yet without sin. Being found in the likeness of sinful flesh He knows no sin, but wears His manhood unpolluted and dwells among men blameless and harmless, the Son of God, without rebuke. Like a sunbeam passing through foul water untarnished and unstained; or like some sweet spring rising in the midst of the salt sea, which yet retains its freshness and pours it over the surrounding bitterness, so Christ takes upon Himself our nature and lays hold of our stained hands with the hand that continues pure while it grasps us, and will make us purer if we grasp it.

Brethren! Let your touch answer to His; and as He lays hold of us, in His incarnation and His death, let the hand of our faith clasp His outstretched hand, and though our hold be as faltering and feeble as that of the trembling, wasted fingers which one timid woman once laid on His garment's hem, the blessing which we need will flow into our veins from the contact. There will be cleansing for our leprosy, sight for our blindness, life driving out death from his throne in our hearts, and we shall be able to recount our joyful experience in the old Psalmist's triumphant strains—"He sent [me] from above, He laid hold upon me, he drew me out of many waters."

IV. Finally we may look upon these incidents as being in a very important sense a pattern for us.

No good is to be done by any man to his fellows except at the cost of true sympathy which leads to identification and contact. The literal touch of your hand would do more good to some poor outcasts than much solemn advice, or even much material help flung to them as from a height above them. A shake of the hand might be more of a means of grace than a sermon, and more comforting than ever so many free breakfasts and blankets given superciliously.

And, symbolically, we may say that we must be willing to take those by the hand whom we wish to help; that is to say, we must come down to their level, try to see with their eyes, and to think their thoughts, and let them feel that we do not think our purity too fine to come beside their filth, nor shrink from them with repugnance, however we may show disapproval and pity for their sin. Much work done by Christian people has no effect, nor ever will have, because it has peeping through it a poorly concealed "I am holier than thou." An instinctive movement of repugnance has ruined many a well-meant effort.

Christ has come down to us, and has taken all our nature upon Himself. If there is an outcast and abandoned soul on earth which may not feel that Jesus has laid a loving and healing touch on him, Jesus is not the Saviour for the world. He shrinks from none; He unites Himself with all; therefore He is able to save to the uttermost all who come unto God by Him.

His conduct is the pattern and the law for us. A Church is a poor affair if it be not a body of people whose experience of Christ's pity and gratitude for the life which has become theirs through His wondrous making Himself one with them, compel them to do the like in their degree for the sinful and the outcast. Thank God! there are many in every communion who know that constraint of the love of Christ! But the world will not be healed of its sickness till the great body of Christian people awakes to feel that the task and honor of each of them is to go forth bearing Christ's pity certified by their own.

The sins of professing Christian countries are largely to be laid at the door of the Church. We are idle when we ought to be at work. We pass by on the other side when bleeding brethren lie with wounds gaping to be bound up by us. And even when we are moved to service by Christ's love, and try to do something for them and for our fellows, our work is often tainted by a sense of our own superiority, and we patronize when we should sympathise, and lecture when we should beseech.

We must be content to take lepers by the hand, if we would help them to purify, and to let every outcast feel the warmth of our pitying, loving grasp, if we would draw them into the forsaken Father's House. Lay your hands on the sinful as Christ did, and they shall recover. All your holiness and hope come from Christ's laying hold of you. Keep hold of Him, and make His great pity and loving identification of Himself with the world of sinners and sufferers your pattern as well as your hope, and your touch, too, will have virtue. Keeping hold of Him Who has taken hold of us, you, too, may be able to say "Ephphatha, be opened," or to lay your hand on the leper and he shall be cleansed.

Almighty God! Who hidest in Thy hand all good, and dost out of Thy full heart give that which we most need when we desire it; we beseech Thee for clean hearts. We pray that we may choose Thee for our portion, and firmly adhere to the choice amid all temptations and difficulties. So shall all things be on our side, and all things yield to us their sweetest sweetness and their highest good.

The Lord be with us in each place and work where His providence has set us to earn our daily bread, and do our daily duty; of whatever kind that may be, whether great or small, whether welcome or unwelcome, may we be ready for it, and find that in doing what we ought there is great reward.

We beseech Thee to keep us from the temptations of our callings, from the weakness of our characters, from all in our circumstances that is meant to test, and may hinder, our faith and love. We beseech Thee that if any of us are bearing any special burden of care or sorrow, of responsibility or duty, Thou wouldst be with such. We commend to Thee sad hearts, we pray for all disappointed ones, for all who are learning how fleeting are our earthly joys, and how only God lasts, and is enough for a man.

Hear us now, O Father! forgive our many sins; grant us Thy gracious help and presence whilst we worship, through Jesus Christ our Lord and Saviour. Amen.[2]

---

[2] From *Pulpit Prayers*.

ONE STEP AT A TIME [1]

We may have the Divine guidance, if we will; in sober reality we have God's presence; and waiting hearts which have ceased from self-will may receive leading as real as ever the pillar gave to Israel.

God's providence does still shape our paths, and God's Spirit will direct us within, and God's word will counsel us. If we will wait and watch we shall not be left undirected. It is wonderful how much practical wisdom about the smallest perplexities of daily life comes to men who keep both their feet and their wishes still until Providence—or, as the world prefers to call it, "circumstances"—clears a path for them. No doubt in all our lives there come times when we seem to have been brought into a blind alley, and cannot see where we are to get out; but it is very rare, indeed, that we do not see one step in advance, the duty which lies next us.

And be sure of this, that if we are content to see but one step at a time, and take it, we shall find our way made plain. The river winds, and often we seem on a lake without an exit. Then is the time to go half-speed, and, doubtless, when we get a little farther, the overlapping hills on either bank will part, and the gorge will open out. We do not need to see it a mile off; enough if we see it when we are close upon it. It may be as narrow and grim, with slippery black cliffs towering on either side of the narrow ribbon of the stream, as the cayons of American rivers, but it will float our boat into broader reaches and onward to the great sea.

[1] From *Similes and Figures from Alexander Maclaren,* by Francis E. Clark. Copyright, 1910, by Fleming H. Revell, and reprinted by permission.

18. DEATH, THE FRIEND [1]

"All things are yours . . . death." I Cor. 3:21, 22.

What Jesus Christ is to a man settles what everything else is to Him. Our relation to Jesus determines our relation to the universe. If we belong to Him, everything belong to us. If we are His servants, all things are our servants. The household of Jesus, which is the whole Creation, is not divided against itself, and the fellow servants do not beat one another. Two bodies moving in the same direction, and under the impulse of the same force, cannot come into collision, and since "all things work together," according to the counsel of His will, "all things work together for good" to His lovers. The triumphant words of my text are no piece of empty rhetoric, but the plain result of two facts—Christ's rule and the Christian's submission. "All things are yours . . . And ye are Christ's." So the stars in their courses fight against those who fight against Him, and if we are at peace with Him we shall "make a league with the beasts of the field, and the stones of the field," which otherwise would be hindrances and stumbling-blocks, "shall be at peace with" us.

The Apostle carries his confidence in the subservience of all things to Christ's servants very far, and the words of my text, in which he dares to suggest that "the Shadow feared of man" is, after all, a veiled friend, are hard to believe, when we are brought face to face with death, either when we meditate on our own end, or when our hearts are sore and our hands are empty. Then the question comes, and often is asked with tears of blood, is it true that this awful force, which we cannot command, does indeed serve us? Did it serve those whom it dragged from our sides; and in serving them, did it serve us? Paul rings out his "Yes"; and if we have as firm a hold of Paul's Lord as Paul had, our answer will be the same. Let me, then, deal with this great thought that lies here, of the

[1] From *Last Sheaves,* American Tract Society, 1904. Reprinted by permission.

conversion of the last enemy into a friend, the assurance that we may all have that death is ours, though not in the sense that we can command it, yet in the sense that it ministers to our highest good.

That thought may be true about ourselves when it comes to our turn to die, and, thank God, has been true about all those that have departed in His faith and fear. Some of you may have seen two very striking engravings by a great, though somewhat unknown artist, representing Death as the Destroyer and Death as the Friend. In the one case he comes into a scene of wild revelry, and there at his feet lie, stark and stiff, corpses in their gay clothing, and with garlands on their brows, and feasters and musicians are flying in terror from the cowled Skeleton. In the other he comes into a quiet church belfry, where an aged saint sits with folded arms, and closed eyes, and an open Bible by his side, and endless peace upon the wearied face. The window is flung wide to the sunrise, and on its sill perches a bird that gives forth its morning song. The cowled figure has brought rest to the weary, and the glad dawning of a new life to the aged, and is a friend. Tho two pictures are better than all the poor words that I can say. It depends on the people to whom he comes, whether he comes as a destroyer or as a helper. Of course, for all of us the mere physical facts remain the same, the pangs and the pain, the slow torture of the loosing of the bond, or the sharp agony of its instantaneous rending apart. But we have gone but a very little way into life and its experiences if we have not learnt that identity of circumstances may cover profound difference of essentials, and that the same experiences may have wholly different messages and meanings to two people who are equally implicated in them. Thus, while the physical fact remains the same for all, the whole bearing of it may so differ that Death to one man will be a Destroyer, while to another it is a Friend. For, if we come to analyze the thoughts of humanity about the last act in human life on earth, what is it that makes the dread darkness of death, which all men know, though they so seldom think of it?

I suppose, first of all, if we seek to question our feelings, that which makes Death a Foe to the ordinary experience is that it is like a step off the edge of a precipice in a fog; a step into a dim condition of which the Imagination can form no conception, because it has no experience, and all Imagination's pictures are painted with pigments drawn from our past. Because it is impossible for a man to have any clear vision of what it is that is coming to meet him, and he cannot tell "in that sleep what dreams may come," he shrinks, as we all shrink, from a step into the vast Inane, the dim Unknown. But the Gospel comes and says, "It *is* a land of great darkness," but "to the people that sit in darkness a great light hath shined."

> Our knowledge of that life is small,
> The eye of faith is dim.

But faith has an eye, and there is light, and this we can see—one Face Whose brightness scatters all the gloom, one Person Who has not ceased to be the Sun of Righteousness with healing in His beams, even in the darkness of the grave. Therefore, one at least of the repellent features which, to the timorous heart, makes Death a foe, is gone, when we know that the known Christ fills the Unknown.

Then, again, another of the elements, as I suppose, which constitute the hostile aspect that Death assumes to most of us, is that it apparently hales us away from all the wholesome activities and occupations of life, and bans us into a state of apparent inaction. The thought that death is rest does sometimes attract the weary or harassed, or they fancy it does, but that is a morbid feeling, and much more common in sentimental epitaphs than among the usual thoughts of men. To most of us there is no joy, but a chill, in the anticipation that all the forms of activity which have so occupied, and often enriched, our lives here, are to be cut off at once. "What am I to do if I have no books?" says the student. "What am I to do if I have no mill?" says the spinner. "What am I to do if I have no nursery or kitchen?" say the women. What are you to do? There is only one quieting answer to such questions. It tells us that what we are doing here is learning our trade, and that we are to be moved into another workshop there, to practice it. Nothing can bereave us of the force we made our own, being here; and "there is nobler work for us to do" when the Master of all the servants stoops from His Throne and says: "Thou hast been faithful over a few things, I will make thee ruler over many things; have thou authority over ten cities." Then the faithfulness of the steward will be exchanged for the authority of the ruler, and the toil of the servant for a share in the joy of the Lord.

So another of the elements which make Death an Enemy is turned into an element which makes it a Friend, and instead of the separation from this earthly body, the organ of our activity and the medium of our connection with the external Universe, being the condemnation of the naked spirit to inaction, it is the emancipation of the spirit into greater activity. For nothing drops away at death that does not make a man the richer for its loss, and when the dross is purged from the silver, there remains "a vessel unto honour ... fit for the Master's use." This mightier activity is the contribution to our blessedness which Death makes to them who use their activities here in Christ's service.

Then, still further, another of the elements which is converted from being a terror into a joy is that Death, the Separator, becomes to Christ's servants Death, the Uniter. We all know how that function of death is perhaps the one that makes us shrink from it the most, dread it the most, and sometimes hate it the most. But it will be with us as it was with those that were to be initiated into ancient religious rites. Blindfolded, they were led by a hand that grasped theirs but was not seen, through dark, narrow, devious passages, but they were led into a great company in a mighty hall. Seen from this side, the ministry of Death parts a man from dear ones, but, Oh! if we could see round the turn in the corridor, we should see that the solitude is but for a moment, and that the true office of Death is not so much to part from those beloved on earth as to carry to, and unite with, Him that is best Beloved in the heavens, and in Him with all His saints. They that are joined to Christ, as they who pass from earth are joined, are thereby joined to all who, in like manner, are knit to Him. Although other dear bonds are loosed by the bony fingers of the Skeleton, his very loosing of them ties more closely the bond that unites us to Jesus, and when the dull ear of the dying has ceased to hear the voices of earth that used to thrill it in their lowest whisper, I suppose it hears another Voice that says: "When thou passest through the fire I will be with thee; and through the waters they shall not overwhelm thee." Thus the Separator unites, first to Jesus, and then to "the general assembly and church of the firstborn," and leads into the city of the living God, the pilgrims who long have lived, often isolated, in the desert.

There is a last element in Death which is changed for the Christian, and that is that to men generally, when they think about it, there is an instinctive recoil from Death, because there is an instinctive suspicion that after Death is the Judgment, and that, somehow or other—never mind about the drapery in which the idea may be embodied for our weakness—when a man dies he passes to a state where he will reap the consequences of what he has sown here. But to Christ's servant that last thought is robbed of its sting, and all the poison sucked out of it, for he can say: "He that died for me makes it possible for me to die undreading, and to pass thither, knowing that I shall meet as my Judge Him Whom I have trusted as my Saviour, and so may have boldness before Him in the Day of Judgment."

Knit these four contrasts together. Death as a step into a dim unknown *versus* Death as a step into a region lighted by Jesus; Death as the cessation of activity *versus* Death as the introduction to nobler opportunities, and the endowment with nobler capacities of service; Death as the Separator and Isolator *versus* Death as uniting to Jesus and all His lovers; Death as haling us to the judgment seat of the adversary *versus* Death as bringing us to the tribunal of the Christ; and I think we can understand how Christians can venture to say, "All things are ours, whether life or death" which lead to a better life.

And now let me add one word more. All this that I have been saying, and all the blessed strength for ourselves and calming in our sorrows which result therefrom, stand or fall with the Resurrection of Jesus Christ. There is nothing else that makes these things certain. There are, of course, instincts, peradventures, hopes, fears, doubts. But in this region, and in regard to all this cycle of truths, the same thing applies which applies round the whole horizon of Christian Revelation—if you want not speculations but certainties, you have to go to Jesus Christ for them. There were many men that thought there were islands of the sea away beyond the setting sun that dyed the western waves, but Columbus went and came back again, and brought their products—and then the thought became a fact. Unless you believe that Jesus Christ has come back from "the bourne from which no traveler returns," and has come laden with the gifts of "happy isles of Eden" far beyond the sea, there is no certitude upon which a dying man can lay his head, or by which a bleeding heart can be staunched. But when He draws near, alive from the dead, and says to us, as He did to the disciples on the evening of the day of Resurrection, "Peace be unto you," and shows us His hands and His side, then we do not only speculate or think a future life possible or probable, or hesitate to deny it, or hope or fear, as the case may be, but we *know,* and we can say: "All things are ours . . . death" amongst others.

The fact that Jesus Christ has died changes the whole aspect of death to His servant, inasmuch as in that great solitude he has a companion, and in the valley of the shadow of death sees footsteps that tell him of One that went before. Nor need I do more than remind you how the manner of our Lord's death shows that He is Lord not only of the dead but of the Death that makes them dead. For His own tremendous assertion, "I have power to lay down [my life], and I have power to take it again," was confirmed by His attitude and His words at the last, as is hinted at by the very expressions with which the Evangelists record the fact of His death: "He yielded up his spirit," "He gave up the ghost," "He breathed out his life." It is confirmed to us by such words as those remarkable ones of the Apocalypse, which speak of Him as "the Living One," who, by His own will, "became dead." He died because He would, and He would die because He loved you and me. And in dying, He showed Himself to be, not the Victim, but the Conqueror, of the Death to which He submitted. The Jewish king on the fatal field of Gilboa called his sword-bearer, and the servant came, and Saul bade him smite, and when his trembling hand shrank from such an act, the king fell on his sword. The Lord of life and death summoned His servant Death, and he came obedient, but Jesus died not by Death's stroke, but by his own act. So that Lord of Death, who died because He would, is the Lord who has the keys of death and the grave, and in regard to one servant says, "I will that he tarry till I come," and that man lives through a century, and in regard to another says, "Follow thou me," and that man dies on a cross. The dying Lord is Lord of Death, and the living Lord is for us all the Prince of Life.

Brethren, we have to take His yoke upon us by the act of faith which leads to a love that issues in an obedience which will become more and more complete, as we become more fully Christ's. Then Death will be ours, for then we shall count that the highest good for us will be fuller union with, a fuller possession of, and a completer conformity to, Jesus Christ our King, and that whatever brings us these, even though it brings also pain and sorrow and much from which we shrink, is all on our side. It is possible—may it be so with each of us!—that for us Death may be, not an enemy that bans us into darkness and inactivity, or hales us to a judgment seat, but the Angel who wakes us, at whose touch the chains fall off, and who leads us through "the iron gate that opens of its own accord," and brings us into the City.

O Lord! grant that we too may rise from the death of self and sin, and may enter into the hidden and heavenly life of Christ, even whilst we are here below. We bless Thee for the victory over foes and fears, for the assurances that He Who is bone of our bone, and flesh of our flesh, has gone to prepare a place for us, and that in His exaltation we are exalted. We thank Thee for the life which comes from that risen Lord Who dwells in all the humble hearts that try to trust in Him, and aspire after closer communion and truer faith. We pray that we too may partake in that life which hath died to sin and lives to God. Oh! purge our hearts, we pray Thee, from all their foolish wanderings away from Thee, and bring us, with settled purpose, with lowly resolution, with grateful surrender, and with triumphant faith to live the lives that we live in the flesh by the faith of the Son of God.

We bless Thee for all Thy providence to us; we would include in our thankfulness all the way by which the Lord our God has led us, even though often it has been in valleys of the Shadow of Death, and amidst places rough and difficult. Yet, Lord, we thank Thee, and we believe that when we see in Heaven we shall praise the road.

We pray Thee to hear us, to forgive all our unworthiness and our many transgressions, for the sake of Jesus Christ our Saviour. Amen.[2]

---

[2] From *Pulpit Prayers*.

THE REWARD OF LOVE [1]

All true love is glad when it is met, glad to give, and glad to receive. Was it not a joy to Jesus to be waited on by the ministering woman? Would He not thank them because they served Him for love? I trow, yes. And if any one stumbles at the word "grateful" as applied to Him, we do not care about the word so long as it is seen that His heart was gladdened by loving friends, and that He recognized in their society a ministry of love.

Notice, too, the loving estimate of what these disciples had done. Their companionship had been imperfect enough at the best. They had given Him but blind affection, dashed with much selfishness. In an hour or two they would all have forsaken Him and fled. He knew all that was lacking in them, and the cowardly abandonment which was so near. But He has not a word to say of all this. He does not count jealously the flaws in our work, or reject it because it is incomplete. So here is the great truth clearly set forth, that where there is a loving heart, there is acceptable service. It is possible that our poor, imperfect deeds shall be an odor of a sweet smell, acceptable, well-pleasing to Him. Which of us that is a father is not glad at his children's gifts, even though they be purchased with his own money, and be of little use? They mean love, so they are precious.

---

[1] From *Similes and Figures from Alexander Maclaren,* by Francis E. Clark. Copyright, 1910, by Fleming H. Revell, and reprinted by permission.

19. WITHOUT THE CAMP [1]

"Let us go forth therefore unto him without the camp, bearing his reproach. For here have we no continuing city, but we seek one to come." HEB. 13:13, 14.

Calvary was outside Jerusalem. That wholly accidental and trivial circumstance is laid hold of in the context, in order to give picturesque force to the main contention and purpose of this Epistle. One of the solemn parts of the ritual of Judaism was the great Day of Atonement, on which the sacrifice that took away the sins of the nation was borne outside the camp, and consumed by fire, instead of being partaken of by the priests, as were most of the other sacrifices. Our writer here sees in these two roughly parallel things, not an argument but an imaginative illustration of great truths. Though he does not mean to say that the death on Calvary was intended to be pointed to by the unique arrangement in question, he does mean to say that the coincidence of the two things helps us to grasp two great truths—one, that Jesus Christ really did what that old sacrifice expressed the need for having done, and the other that, in His death on Calvary, the Jewish nation, as one of the parables has it, "cast him out of the vineyard." In the context, he urges this analogy between the two things.

But a Christ outside the camp beckons His disciples to His side. If any man serve Him, he has to follow Him, and the blessedness, as well as the duty, of the servant on earth, as well as in heaven, is to be where his Master is. So the writer finds here a picturesque way to enforce the great lesson of his treatise, namely, that the Jewish adherent to Christianity must break with Judaism. In the early stages, it was possible to combine faith in Christ and adherence to the Temple and its ritual. But now that by process of time and experience the Church has learnt better

---
[1] From *Last Sheaves*, American Tract Society, 1904. Reprinted by permission.

Who and What Christ is, that which was in part has to be done away, and the Christian Church is to stand clear of the Jewish synagogue.

Now it is to be distinctly understood that the words of my text, in the writer's intention, are not a general principle or exhortation, but that they are a special commandment to a certain class under special circumstances, and when we use them, as I am going to do now, for a wider purpose, we must remember that that wider purpose was by no means in the writer's mind. What he was thinking about was simply the relation between the Jewish Christian and the Jewish community. But if we take them as we may legitimately do—only remembering that we are diverting them from their original intention—as carrying more general lessons for us, what they seem to teach is that faithful discipleship involves detachment from the world. This commandment, "Let us go forth unto him without the camp," stands, if you will notice, between two reasons for it, which buttress it up, as it were, on either side. Before it is enunciated, the writer has been pointing, as I have tried to show, to the thought that a Christ without the camp necessarily involves disciples without the camp. And he follows it with another reason, "Here we have no continuing city, but we seek that which is to come." Here, then, is a general principle, supported on either side by a great reason.

Let me first try to set before you—

The Jewish Christian was obliged utterly and outwardly to break his connection with Judaism, on the peril, if he did not, of being involved in its ruin, and, as was historically the case with certain Judaizing sects, of losing his Christianity altogether. It was a cruel necessity, and no wonder that it needed this long letter to screw the disciples of Hebrew extraction up to the point of making the leap from the sinking ship to the deck of the one that floated. The parallel does not hold with regard to us. The detachment from the world, or the coming out from the camp, to which my text exhorts, is not the abandonment of our relations with what the Bible calls "the world," and what we call—roughly meaning the same thing—society. The function of the Christian Church as leaven, involved the necessity of being closely associated, and in contact with, all forms of human life, national, civic, domestic, social, commercial, intellectual, political. Does my text counsel an opposite course? "Go forth without the camp"—does that mean huddle yourself together into a separate flock, and let the camp go to the devil? By no means. For the society or world, out of which the Christian is drawn by the attraction of the Cross, like iron filings out of a heap by a magnet, is in itself good and God-appointed. It is He "that setteth the solitary in families." It is He that gathers humanity into the bonds of civic and national life. It is He that gives capacities which find their sphere, their education, and their increase, in the walks of intellectual, or commercial, or political life. And He does not build up with one hand and destroy with the other, or set men by His providence in circumstances out of which He draws them by His grace. By no means. To go apart from humanity is to miss the very purpose for which God has set the Church in the world. For contact with the sick to be healed is requisite for healing, and they are poor disciples of the "Friend of publicans and sinners" who prefer to consort with Pharisees. "Let both grow together till the harvest"—the roots are intertwined, and it is God that has intertwined them.

Now, I know that one does not need to insist upon this principle to the average Christianity of this day, which is only too ready to mingle itself with the world, but one does need to insist that, in so mingling, detachment from the world is still to be observed; and it does need to be taught that Christian men are not lowering the standard of the Christian life, when they fling themselves frankly and energetically into the various forms of human activity, if and only if, whilst they do so, they still remember and obey the commandment, "Let us go forth unto him without the camp." The commandment misinterpreted so as to be absolutely impossible to be obeyed, becomes a snare to people who do not keep it, and yet sometimes feel as if they were to blame, because they do not. And, therefore, I turn in the next place to consider—

II. What this detachment really is.

Will you let me put what I have to say into the shape of two or three plain, practical exhortations, not because I wish to assume a position of authority or command, but only in order to give vividness and point to my thoughts?

First, then, let us habitually nourish the inner life of union with Jesus Christ. Notice the words of my text, and see what comes first and what comes second. "Let us go forth unto him"—that is the main thing. "Without the camp" is second, and a consequence; "unto him," is primary, which is just to say that the highest, widest, noblest, all-comprehensive conception of what a Christian life is, is that it is union with Jesus Christ and whatever else it is follows from that. The soul is ever to be looking up through all the shadows and shows, the changes and circumstances, of this fleeting present unto Him, and seeking to be more closely united with Him. Union with Him is life, and separation from Him is death. To be so united is to be a Christian. Never mind about camps or anything else, to begin with. If the heart is joined to Jesus, then all the rest will come right. If it is not, then you may make regulations as many as you like, and they will be only red tape to entangle your feet in. "Let us go forth unto him"; that is the sovereign commandment. And how is that to be done? How is it to be done but by nourishing habitual consciousness of union with Him and life in Him, by an habitual reference of all our acts to Him? As the Roman Catholics put it, in their hard, external way, "the practice of the Presence of God" is the keynote to all real, vigorous Christianity. For, brethren, such an habitual fellowship with Jesus Christ is possible for us. Though with many interruptions, not doubt, still ideally it is possible that it shall be a great deal more continuous than, alas! it is with many of us.

Depend upon it, this nourishing of an inward life of fellowship with Jesus, so that we may say "our lives are hid"—hid, after all vigorous manifestations and consistent action—"with Christ in God," will not weaken, but increase, the force with which we act on the things seen and temporal. There is an unwholesome kind of mysticism which withdraws men from the plain duties of everyday life; and there is a deep, sane, wholesome, and eminently Christian mysticism which enable men to come down with greater force, and to act with more decision, with more energy, with more effect, in all common deeds of life. The greatest mystics have been the hardest workers. Who was it that said, "I live; yet not I, but Christ liveth in me?" That man had gone far, very far toward a habitual consciousness of Christ's presence, and it was the same man that said, "That which cometh upon me daily, the care of all the churches." The greatest mystic of the Middle Ages, the saint that rode by the lake all day long, and was so absorbed in contemplation that he said at night, "Where is the lake?" was the man that held all the threads of European politics in his hands, and from his cell at Clairvaux guided popes, and flung the nations of the West into a Crusade. John Wesley was one of the hardest workers that the Church has ever had, and was one of those who lived most habitually without the camp. Be sure of this, that the more our lives are wrapped in Christ, the more energetic will they be in the world. They tell us that the branches of a spreading tree describe roughly the same circumference in the atmosphere that its roots do underground, and so far as our roots extend in Christ, so far will our branches spread in the world. "Let us go forth unto him without the camp."

Again, let me say, do the same things as other people, but with a difference. The more our so-called civilization advances, the more, I was going to say, mechanical, or at least largely released from the control of the will and the personal idiosyncrasy, become great parts of our work. The Christian weaver drives her looms very much in the same fashion that the non-Christian girl who is looking after the next set does. The Christian clerk adds up his figures, and writes his letters, very much in the same fashion that the worldly clerk does. The believing doctor visits his patients, and writes out his prescriptions in the fashion that his neighbor who is not a Christian does. But there is always room for the personal equation—always!—and two lives may be, superficially and roughly, the same, and yet there may be a difference in them impalpable, undefinable, but very obvious, and very real, and very mighty. The Christian motive is love to Jesus Christ and fellowship with Him, and that motive may be brought to bear upon all life—

> A servant with this clause
> Makes drudgery divine.

He that for Christ's sake does a common thing lifts it out of the fatal region of the commonplace, and makes it great and beautiful. We do not want from all Christian people specifically Christian service, in the narrow sense which the phrase has acquired, half so much as we want common things done from an uncommon motive; worldly things done because of the love of Jesus Christ in our hearts. And, depend upon it, just as, from some unseen bank of violets, there come odors in opening spring, so from the unspoken and deeply hidden motive of love to Jesus Christ, there will be a fragrance in our commonest actions which all men recognize. They tell us that rivers which flow from lakes are so clear that they are tinged throughout with celestial blue, because all the mud that they brought down from their upper reaches has been deposited in the still waters of the lake from which they flow; and if from the deep tarn of love to Jesus Christ in our hearts the stream of our lives flows out, it will be like the Rhone below Geneva, distinguishable from the muddy waters that run by its side in the same channel. Two people, partners in business, joined in the same work, marching step for step in the same ranks, may yet be entirely distinguishable and truly separate, because, doing the same things, they do them from different motives.

Let me say, still further, and finally about this matter, that sometimes we shall have to come actually out of the camp. The world as God made it is good; society is ordained by God. The occupations which men pursue are of his appointment, for the most part. But into the thing that was good there have crept all manner of corruptions and abominations, so that often it will be a Christian duty to come away from all outward connection with that which is incurably corrupt. I know very well that a morality which mainly consists of prohibitions is pedantic and poor. I know very well that a Christianity which interprets such a precept as this of my text simply as meaning abstinence from certain conventionally selected and branded forms of life, occupation, or amusement, is but a very poor affair. But "Thou shalt not" is very often absolutely necessary as a support to "Thou shalt." If you go into an Eastern city, you will find the houses with their fronts to the street, having narrow slits of windows all barred, and a heavy gate, frowning and ugly. But pass within, and there are flower beds and fountains. The frowning street front is there for the defense of the fountains and flower beds within, from the assaults of foes, and speaks of a disturbed state of society, in which no flowers can grow and no fountains can bubble and sparkle, unless a strong barrier is round them. And so "thou shalt not," in a world like this, is needful in order that "thou shalt" shall have fair play. No law can be laid down for other people. Every man must settle this matter of abstinence for himself. Things that you may do, perhaps I may not do; things that you may not do, I very rightly may. "A liberal Christianity," as the world calls it, is often a very shallow Christianity. "A sour Puritanical severity," as loose-living men call it, is very often plain, Christian morality. An inconsistent Christian may be hailed as "a good fellow," and laughed at behind his back. Samson made sport for the Philistines when he was blind. The uncircumcised do often say of professing Christians, that try to be like them and keep step with them, "What do these Hebrews here?" and God always says to such, "What dost thou here, Elijah?"

Lastly—

III. Why this detachment is enforced.

"For here we have no continuing city, but we seek *one to come.*" That translation does not give the full force of the original, for it suggests the idea of a vague uncertainty in the seeking, whereas what the writer means is, not "one to come," but *one which is coming.* The Christian object of seeking is definite, and it is not merely future, but present and in process of being realized even here and now, and tending to completion. Paul uses the same metaphor of the city in one of his letters, "Our citizenship is in heaven." He says that to the Philippians. Philippi was a colony; that is to say, it was a bit of Rome put down in a foreign land, with Roman laws, its citizens enrolled upon the registers of the Roman tribes, and not under the jurisdiction of the provincial governor. That is what we Christians are, whether we know it or not. We are here in an order to which we outwardly belong, but in the depths of our being we belong to another order of things altogether. Therefore the essentials of the Christian life may be stated as being the looking forward to the city, and the realizing of our affinities with it and not with the things around us. In the measure in which, dear brethren, we realize to what community we belong, will the things here be seen to be fleeting and alien to our deepest selves. "Here we have no continuing city" is not merely the result of the transiency of temporal things, and the brevity of our earthly lives, but it is much rather the result of our vivid realization and continual anticipation of, and our affinity with, the other order of things beyond the seas.

Abraham dwelt in tents, because he "looked for a city," and so it was better for him to stop on the breezy uplands, though the herbage was scant, than to go down with Lot into the vale of Sodom, though it looked like the garden of the Lord. In like manner, the more intensely we realize that we belong to the city, the more shall we be willing to "go forth without the camp." Let these two thoughts dominate our minds and shape our lives; our union with Jesus Christ and our citizenship of the heavenly Jerusalem. In the measure in which they do, it will be no sacrifice for us to come out of the transient camp, because we shall thereby go to Him, and come to the City of the living God, the heavenly Jerusalem, "which hath the foundations."

O Lord, our God! we do come unto Thy house; in the multitude of Thy mercies help us to worship in Thy fear toward Thy holy Temple, and lift up our hearts, we beseech Thee, to Thee now.

We beseech Thee to keep us from our own besetting sins, from our own particular temptations, from those things which may make the strongest appeal to our worst parts, from all the difficulties and temptations belonging to our professions or occupations, to our temperament or to circumstances. Thou knowest what these are, and we thank Thee for all the Fatherly pity with which Thou dost look on Thy feeble children, and we pray Thee that Thou wouldst strengthen us there where Thou knowest that we are weakest, and where we sometimes know not that we are. Help us day by day in the routine of our daily duties. May we not reckon anything as of little importance because we do it every day we live. May the things that we have done oftenest be done best, and in all of them may we keep up the freshness of feeling that we have not passed this way heretofore, and that God is with us, to make all things—even old tasks, and commonplace duties, and familiar, life-long associations—all things new.

Lead us by Thy light; deliver us from temptation; set our feet upon a Rock; and establish our goings that we may all behold wondrous things out of Thy law, and go away quickened and strengthened and brought nearer to Christ. Amen.[2]

---
[2] From *Pulpit Prayers*.

DREAMS AND DEEDS [1]

Have you realized how different it is to dream things and to do them? In our dreams we are, as it were, working in vacuo. When we come to acts, the atmosphere offers resistance. It is easy to imagine ourselves victorious in circumstances where things are all going rightly and are blending according to our own desires; but when we come to the grim world, where there are things that resist and people are not plastic, it is a very different matter. You do not yet understand, as you will someday, the fatal limitations of power that hem us all in, and the obstinate way that circumstances have of not falling in with our wishes. And you have not yet learned how completely and constantly failure accompanies success, like its shadow. The old Egyptians had no need to put a skeleton at the tables, nor the Romans to set mocker behind the hero as he rode in triumph up to the Capitol. The world provides the skeleton at the banquet, and circumstances supply the mocker to add a dash of failure to all our triumphs.

[1] From *Similes and Figures from Alexander Maclaren*, by Francis E. Clark. Copyright, 1910, by Fleming H. Revell, and reprinted by permission.

20. WHAT LASTS [1]

"Whether there be prophecies, they shall fail; whether there be tongues, they shall cease; whether there be knowledge, it shall vanish away . . . And now abideth faith, hope, charity, these three . . ." I COR. 13:8, 13.

We discern the run of the Apostle's thought best by thus omitting the intervening verses and connecting these two. The part omitted is but a buttress of what has been stated in the former of our two verses; and when we thus unite them there is disclosed plainly the Apostle's intention of contrasting two sets of things, three in each. The one set is prophecies, tongues, knowledge; the other, faith, hope, charity. There also comes out distinctly that the point mainly intended by the contrast is the transiency of the one and the permanence of the other. Now, that contrast has been obscured and weakened by two mistakes, about which I must say a word.

With regard to the former statement, "whether there be prophecies, they shall fail; whether there be tongues, they shall cease," that has been misunderstood as if it amounted to a declaration that the miraculous gifts in the early Church were intended to be of brief duration. However true that may be, it is not what Paul means here. The cessation to which he refers is their cessation, in the light of the perfect future. With regard to the other statement, the abiding of faith, hope, charity, that, too, has been misapprehended as if it indicated that faith and hope belonged to this state of things only, and that love was the greatest of the three, because it was permanent. The reason for that misconception has mainly lain in the misunderstanding of the force of *"Now,"* which has been taken to mean "for the present," as an implied contrast to an unspoken "then"; just as in the previous verse we have, *"Now* we see through a

---
[1] From *Triumphant Certainties,* American Baptist Publication Society, 1897.

glass . . . *then* face to face." But the "now" in this text is not, as the grammarians say, temporal, but logical. That is, it does not refer to time, but to the sequence of the Apostle's thought, and is equivalent to "so then." "So then abideth, faith, hope, charity."

The scope of the whole, then, is to contrast the transient with the permanent, in Christian experience. If we firmly grasped the truth involved, our estimates would be rectified and our practice revolutionized.

I. I ask this question: What will drop away?

Paul answers, "prophecies, tongues, knowledge." Now these three are all extraordinary gifts belonging to the present phase of the Christian life. But inasmuch as these gifts were the heightening of natural capacities and faculties, it is perfectly legitimate to enlarge the declaration and to use these three words in their widest signification. So understood, they come to this, that all our present modes of apprehension and of utterance are transient, and will be left behind.

"Knowledge, it shall cease," and as the Apostle goes on to explain, in the verses which I have passed over for my present purpose, it shall cease because the perfect will absorb into itself the imperfect, as the inrushing tide will obliterate the little pools in the rocks on the seashore. For another reason, the knowledge, the mode of apprehension belonging to the present, will pass—because here it is indirect, and there it will be immediate. "We shall know face to face," which is what philosophers call by intuition. Here our "knowledge creeps from point to point," painfully amassing facts, and thence, with many hesitations and errors, groping its way towards principles and laws. Here it is imperfect, with many a gap in the circumference; or like the thin red line on a map which shows the traveler's route across a prairie; or like the spider's thread in the telescope, stretched athwart the blazing disc of the sun—"but then face to face." Incomplete knowledge shall be done away; and many of its objects will drop, and much of what makes the science of earth will be antiquated and effete. What would the handloom weaver's knowledge of how to throw his shuttle be worth in a weaving-shed with a thousand looms? Just so much will the knowledges of earth be when we get yonder.

Modes of utterance will cease. With new experiences will come new methods of communication, as a man can speak, and a beast can only growl or bark. So a man in heaven, with new experiences, will have new methods of communication. The comparison between that mode of utterance which we now have, and that which we shall then possess, will be like the difference between the old-fashioned semaphore, that used to wave about clumsy wooden arms in order to convey intelligence, and the telegraph.

Think, then, of a man going into that future life, and saying, "I knew more about Sanscrit than anybody that ever lived in Europe"; "I sang sweet song"; "I was a past master in philology, grammars, and lexicons"; "I was a great orator." "Tongues shall cease"; and the modes of utterance that belonged to earth, and all that holds of them, will drop away, and be of no more use.

If these things are true, brethren, with regard even to the highest form of these high and noble things, how much more and more solemnly true are they with regard to the aims and objects which most of us have in view. They will all drop away, and we shall be left, stripped of what, for most of us, has made the whole interest and activity of our lives.

II. What will last?

"So then, abideth these three, faith, hope, love." When Paul takes three nouns and couples them with a verb in the singular, he is not making a slip of the pen, or committing a grammatical blunder which a child could correct. But there is a great truth in that piece of apparent grammatical irregularity; for the faith, the hope, and the love, for which he can only afford a singular verb, are thereby declared to be in their depth and essence one thing, and it, the triple star, abides, and continues to shine; the three primitive colors are unified in the white beam of light. Do not correct the grammar, and spoil the sense, but discern what he means when he says, "Now abid*eth* faith, hope, love." For this is what he means, that the two latter come out of the former, and that without it they are nought, and that it without them is dead.

Faith breeds hope. *There* is the difference between earthly hopes and Christian people's hopes. Our hopes, apart from the revelation of God in Jesus Christ, are but the balancing of probabilities, and the scale is often dragged down by the clutch of eager desires. But all is baseless and uncertain, unless our hopes are the outcome of our faith. Which, being translated into other words, is just this, that the one basis on which men can rest—aye! even for the immediate future, and the contingencies of life, as well as for the solemnities and certainties of heaven—any legitimate and substantial hope is trust in Jesus Christ, His word, His love, His power, and for the heavenly future, in His Resurrection and present glory. A man that believes these things, and only that man, has a rock foundation on which he can build his hope.

Faith, in like manner, is the parent of love. Paul and John, diverse as they are in the whole cast of their minds, the one being speculative and the other mystical, the one argumentative and the other simply gazing and telling what he sees, are precisely agreed in regard of this matter. For, to the Apostle of Love, the foundation of all human love toward God is, "we have known and believed the love that God hath to us," and "we love him, because he first loved us." And to Paul the first thing is the trusting reception of the love of God, "commended to us" by the fact that "whilst we were yet sinners, Christ died for us." And from that necessarily flows, if the faith be genuine, the love that answers the sacrifice and obeys the Beloved. So faith, hope, love, these three are a trinity in unity, and it abideth. That is the main point of our last text. Let me say a word or two about it.

I have said that the words have often been misunderstood as if the "now," referred only to the present order of things, in which faith and hope are supposed to find their only appropriate sphere. But that is clearly not the Apostle's meaning here, for many reasons with which I need not trouble you. The abiding of all three is eternal abiding, and there is a heavenly as well as an earthly form of faith and hope as well as of love. Just look at these points for a moment.

"Faith abides," says Paul, yonder, as here. Now, there is a common saying, which I suppose ninety out of a hundred people think comes out of the Bible, about faith being lost in sight. There is no such teaching in Scripture. True, in one aspect, faith is the antithesis of sight. True, Paul does say "we walk by faith, not by sight." But that antithesis refers only to part of faith's significance. In so far as it is the opposite of sight, of course it will cease to be in operation when "we shall know even as we are known," and "see Him as He is." But the essence of faith is not the absence of the person trusted, but the emotion of trust which goes out to the person, present or absent. And in its deepest meaning of absolute dependence and happy confidence, faith abides through all the glories, and the lusters of the heavens, as it burns amidst the dimnesses and the darknesses of earth. Forever and ever, on through the irrevoluble ages of eternity, dependence on God in Christ will be the life of the glorified, as it was the life of the militant Church. No millenniums of possession, and no imaginable increases in beauty, and perfectness, and enrichment with the wealth of God, will bring us one inch nearer to casting off the state of filial dependence which is, and ever will be, the condition of our receiving them all. Faith "abides."

Hope "abides." For it is no more a Scriptural idea that hope is lost in fruition, than it is that faith is lost in sight. Rather, that future presents itself to us as the continual communication of an inexhaustible God to our progressively capacious and capable spirits. In that continual communication there is continual progress. Wherever there is progress there must be hope. And thus the fair form, which has so often danced before us elusive, and has led us into bogs and miry places and then faded away, will move before us through all the long avenues of an endless progress, and will ever and anon come back to tell us of the unseen glories that lie beyond the next turn, and to woo us further into the depths of heaven and the fullness of God. Hope "abides."

Love "abides." I need not, I suppose, enlarge upon that thought which nobody denies, that love is the eternal form of the human relation to God. It, too, like the mercy which it clasps, "endureth forever."

But I may remind you of what the Apostle does not explain in our text, that it is greater than its linked sisters, because whilst faith and hope belong only to a creature, and are dependent and expectant of some good to come to themselves, and correspond to something which is in God in Christ, the love which springs from faith and hope not only corresponds to, but resembles, that from which it comes and by which it lives. The fire kindled is cognate with the fire that kindles; and the love that is in man is like the love that is in God. It is the climax of his nature; it is the fulfilling of all duty; it is the crown and jeweled clasp of all perfection. And so "these three abideth, faith, hope, love, and the greatest of these is love."

III. Lastly, what follows from all this?

First, let us be quite sure that we understand what this abiding love is. I daresay you have heard people say "Ah! I do not care much about Paul's theology. Give me the thirteenth chapter of the first Epistle to the Corinthians. That is beautiful; that praise of love; *that* comes home to men." Yes, very beautiful. Are you sure that you know what Paul means by "love"? I do not use the word "charity," because that lovely word, like a glistening meteor that falls upon the earth, has a rust, as it were, upon its surface that dims its brightness very quickly. Charity has come to mean an indulgent estimate of other people's faults; or, still more degradingly, the giving of money out of your pockets to other people's necessities. These are what the people who do not care much about Paul's theology generally suppose that he means here. But these do not exhaust his meaning. Paul's notion of love is the response of the human love to the Divine, which Divine is received into the heart by simple faith in Jesus Christ. And his notion of love which never faileth, and endureth all things, and hopeth all things, is love to men, which is but one stream of the great river of love to God. If we rightly understand what he means by love, we shall find that his praise of love is as theological as anything that he ever wrote. We shall never get further than barren admiration of a beautiful piece of writing, unless our love to men has the source and root to which Paul points us.

Again, let us take this great thought of the permanence of faith, hope, and love as being the highest conception that we can form of our future condition. It is very easy to bewilder ourselves with speculations and theories of another life. I do not care much about them. The great gates keep their secret well. Few stray beams of light find their way through their crevices. The less we say the less likely we are to err. It is easy to let ourselves be led away, by turning rhetoric into revelation, and accepting the symbols of the New Testament as if they carried anything more than images of the realities. But far beyond golden pavements, and harps, and crowns, and white robes, lies this one great thought that the elements of the imperfect, Christlike life of earth are the essence of the perfect, Godlike life in heaven. "Now abide these three, faith, hope, love."

Last of all, let us shape our lives in accordance with these certainties. The dropping away of the transient things is no argument for neglecting or despising them; for our handling of them makes our characters, and our characters abide. But it is a very excellent argument for shaping our lives so as to seek first the first things, and to secure the permanent qualities, and so to use the transient as that it shall all help us toward that which does not pass.

What will a Manchester man that knows nothing except goods and office work, and knows these only in their superficial aspect, and not as related to God, what, in the name of common sense, will he do with himself when he gets into a world where there is not a single ledger, nor a desk, nor a yard of cloth of any sort? What will some of us do when, in like manner, we are stripped of all the things that we have cared about, and worked for, and have made our aims down here? Suppose you knew that you were under sailing orders to go somewhere or other, and that at any moment a breathless messenger might come in and say, "Come along! we are all waiting for you"; and suppose that you never did a single thing toward getting your outfit ready, or preparing yourself in any way for that which might come at any moment, and could not but come before very long. Would you be a wise man? But that is what a great many of us are doing, doing every day, and all day long, and doing that only. "He shall leave them in the midst of his days," says a grim text, "and at his [latter] end shall be a fool."

What will drop? Modes of apprehension, modes of utterance, occupations, duties, relationships, loves; and we shall be left standing naked, stripped as it were, to the very quick, and only as much left as will keep our souls alive. But if we are clothed with faith, hope, love, we shall not be found naked. Cultivate the high things, the permanent things; then death will not wrench you violently from all that you have been and cared for; but it will usher you into the perfect form of all that you have been and done upon earth. All these things will pass, but faith, hope, love, "stay not behind nor in the grave are trod," but will last as long as Christ, their Object, lives, and as long as we in Him live also.

O Lord, our gracious God! help us to come to Thee feeling that Thou givest all life and breath and all things; and lifting up our hearts to Thee in humble desire. We thank Thee for all Thy mercies to us, and in our thankfulness would pray for grace to embrace all Thy dealings with us, of however diverse sorts they may be. Surely Thou dwellest in the darkness as well as in the light, and Thou sendest the storms that stoop upon our path as well as the sunshine and the calm; and Thou hast made winter as well as summer, and the outgoings of the evening as of the morning to rejoice. Help us to recognize Thy presence in everything; in sorrows and disappointments, in losses and difficulties, in anxieties and trials, all which test our faith, and by (such) testing may we find in Thee a better and an enduring blessedness.

Draw near in Thy tenderness to Christian hearts, and gently bind up the wounded; for Thou only knowest how to heal so as not to hurt; and Thy consolations never wound nor irritate, as our clumsy ones often do.

Hear us in our petitions; forgive our many sins; grant us Thy gracious presence as we bow before Thee, and answer us, for all we ask is through Jesus Christ our Saviour Lord. Amen.[2]

---

[2] From *Pulpit Prayers*.